The International Behavioural and Social Sciences Library

NEW WAYS IN MANAGEMENT TRAINING

TAVISTOCK

The International Behavioural and Social Sciences Library

INDUSTRIAL RELATIONS
In 13 Volumes

I	Efficiency and Effort *W Baldamus*
II	Interdependence and Uncertainty *Edited by Charles Crichton*
III	Form and Content in Industrial Democracy *F E Emery and Einar Thorsrud*
IV	The Dynamics of a Changing Technology *Peter J Fensham and Douglas Hooper*
V	Communications in the Building Industry *Gurth Higgin and Neil Jessop*
VI	The Game of Budget Control *G H Hofstede*
VII	The Changing Culture of a Factory *Elliott Jaques*
VIII	Measurement of Responsibility *Elliott Jaques*
IX	Mid-Career Development *Robert N Rapoport*
X	The Enterprise and its Environment *A K Rice*
XI	Managers *Kenn Rogers*
XII	New Ways in Management Training *Cyril Sofer and Geoffrey Hutton*
XIII	The Enterprise in Transition *H van der Haas*

NEW WAYS IN MANAGEMENT TRAINING

A Technical College Develops its Services to Industry

CYRIL SOFER AND
GEOFFREY HUTTON

Routledge
Taylor & Francis Group
LONDON AND NEW YORK

First published in 1958 by
Tavistock Publications Limited

Published in 2001 by
Routledge
2 Park Square, Milton Park, Abingdon, Oxfordshire OX14 4RN
711 Third Avenue, New York, NY 10017

First issued in paperback 2014

Routledge is an imprint of the Taylor and Francis Group, an informa business

British Library Cataloguing in Publication Data
A CIP catalogue record for this book
is available from the British Library

New Ways in Management Training
ISBN 0-415-26447-2
Industrial Relations: 13 Volumes
ISBN 0-415-26510-X
The International Behavioural and Social Sciences Library
112 Volumes
ISBN 0-415-25670-4

ISBN 13: 978-1-138-86377-4 (pbk)
ISBN 13: 978-0-415-26447-1 (hbk)

CYRIL SOFER
GEOFFREY HUTTON

New Ways in Management Training

A Technical College Develops
its Services to Industry

FOREWORD BY
PROFESSOR W. R. HAWTHORNE

TAVISTOCK PUBLICATIONS LIMITED
2 BEAUMONT STREET, LONDON W1

First published in 1958
by Tavistock Publications Ltd
2 Park Square, Milton Park,
Abingdon, Oxon, OX14 4RN

in 10 point Times Roman type
by East Midland Printing Company
Bury St. Edmunds,
Peterborough and elsewhere

CONTENTS

FOREWORD

In this country and indeed all over the world there is a pressing need for more men and women able to combine technical and professional skills with managerial ability and capacity for leadership. Educational institutions are responding by expanding the teaching of science, both pure and applied, while trying to bridge the present gulf between science and arts teaching. As one special type of response to this need, some have introduced specific training in management, and this has been found of great value toward the development of understanding and competence.

The expansion and the changes in educational programmes resulting from these new demands for training in professional skills present a number of difficulties. Several public committees have studied the problems and much has been done at the administrative level to promote the furtherance of education suited to these modern needs. Education and training are, however, very personal affairs which cannot be promoted successfully by administrative energy alone. The differing ways in which one individual, the teacher, can develop the ideas, attitudes, and skills of another individual, the pupil, are of prime importance and need to be studied and understood.

The Tavistock Institute of Human Relations, whose research has often provided material for management training, has by this study of the development of a department of management and production engineering in a technical college cast new light for educational administrators, industrial managers, and social scientists on problems of management training.

While the material is of major interest to teachers and administrators in every kind of educational establishment, it is natural that the book is of greatest relevance to those involved in the control and development of technical colleges, whose role in professional development is so significant.

The insight offered by the chapters describing and discussing relations between the industrial firms and the college should be stimulating to managers and teachers concerned with education and training. The chapter on the teacher at work is in itself a classic.

The Tavistock Institute has a well-deserved reputation for its development of techniques of collaborative research projects in which the research is carried out jointly by the Institute and the organization studied. Methods of social research suitable for the study of relatively unsophisticated groups have been developed elsewhere. The social scientist will be particularly interested in the discussion of the research approach in this novel operational study of a sophisticated group in an educational establishment.

The authors have distilled from their research a valuable book containing new material which deserves widespread study.

W. R. HAWTHORNE
Professor of Applied Thermodynamics
Department of Engineering
University of Cambridge

PREFACE

The study reported upon in this book was carried out during the years 1954 to 1956 by the Tavistock Institute of Human Relations in collaboration with the Department of Management and Production Engineering at Acton Technical College, London.

It was one of a series sponsored by the Joint Committee on Human Relations in Industry set up by the Department of Scientific and Industrial Research and the Medical Research Council in 1953. The Committee was appointed 'to examine current activities concerning the study of human relations in industry and to call attention to problems of special timeliness and promise on which research, including applied research and field study, might be undertaken or supported by the D.S.I.R., the M.R.C., or other bodies'. The studies included in the D.S.I.R. programme were financed by Counterpart funds derived from United States Economic Aid, and were designed to have a bearing upon the productivity of the country and to produce results not only of enduring scientific interest, but also of relatively short-term utility.

The objectives of the research described in this book were: (i) to examine the function and possibilities of a department of management and production engineering in servicing industry; (ii) to examine with that department its services and structure; (iii) to establish the most effective feed-back mechanism from industry to the department.

These objectives were originally set by the Department of Management and Production Engineering at Acton Technical College, the Head of which made a successful application to the Joint Committee for the necessary funds.

The project could not be started when the grant was first made because of difficulty in arranging who should control it.

Original plans had envisaged that the project would be carried out by a research team employed by the College itself. On further exploration, it was concluded that such an arrangement would be unworkable, largely because the prospective research workers, if employed in such a way, would lack the freedom and objectivity necessary for a candid assessment of the Department.

Protracted negotiations took place over nearly a year between the County Council, the College, possible research workers, and the grant-providing body (the D.S.I.R.-M.R.C. Joint Committee). These negotiations revolved on the one hand round the need of the County Council for security against the disturbance of existing arrangements by irresponsible criticism, and, on the other, around the need of the research workers for a degree of independence sufficient for them to carry out their work in an impartial manner.

The Tavistock Institute was asked to help in these negotiations. The points at issue were clarified at an informal meeting between the Chairman of the County Council, the Chairman of the responsible Education Committee, and the Chairman of the Management Committee of the Tavistock Institute.

Eventually the opinion emerged from the committees and individuals concerned that it would be desirable if the Institute could itself conduct the research. It was felt that the Institute could provide the research workers with an independent base from which they could work with a reasonable degree of scientific freedom and could, in accordance with its usual working arrangements with client organizations, guarantee professional confidentiality in respect of research data until approval could be given to further communication.

Finally, in March 1954, the Middlesex County Council requested the Tavistock Institute to undertake the project. In accordance with the usual practice of the Institute and the bodies with which it undertakes research, arrangements were made regularly to review the work; and the County, the Department of Management and Production Engineering, and the Institute reserved the right to cease the work in the event of their wishing to do so. Experience has shown that such a guarantee helps toward fruitful joint work and towards publication of research results.

The study itself began on 1st June 1954 and ended on 31st May 1956. It was a case study of one technical college department, its students, local firms, and other groups and organizations affecting its work. The matters with which it was concerned were of public importance as well as of local interest within the County of Middlesex and the Borough of Acton; they included the functions of technical institutions in assisting with the quantity and quality of industrial output, the relative roles of universities and technical colleges in training for management and production engineering, the relation of these subjects to other branches of technical college teaching, and the relation of experience to academic instruction in the training of managers.

Although the research grant that financed the research expired on 31st May 1956, the Institute found it necessary to continue for a while on its own funds to complete a final report and discuss it with the various interested people. The report was completed and agreed with the Management Department by the end of 1956, and was finally cleared by the College and County Council by April 1957.

Three full-length interim progress reports were completed by the Tavistock Institute at approximately six-monthly intervals during the research and thoroughly discussed with the individuals and groups concerned. The object was to make emerging material available during the project, so that its practical implications could be explored immediately. At the same time the Tavistock Institute used emerging findings to help the Management Department with the practical developmental matters described in detail in the book.

This book is, therefore, a report on work done by the Institute with the Department, as well as a report on facts discovered during the research.

The generalizations in this book are based on several sources of information in addition to the case study. These sources include relevant literature and press comments, Ministry and Middlesex County Council regulations and circulars; interviews with representatives of technical colleges other than Acton, local authority and Ministry officials, and professional associations; observations and interviews with firms and students; and the Tavistock Institute's experience and knowledge of management training, industrial operations, and advisory work.

Our thanks are due to the Middlesex County Council Education Committee and Research Project Sub-Committee; the Assistant Education Officer for Further Education; the present Principal, his predecessor, and the Chairman and Governing Body of Acton Technical College.

We are especially grateful to the full-time teaching staff of the Department of Management and Production Engineering, Mr. R. A. F. Harcourt (Head), Mr. L. H. Hancock, Mr. S. H. Freemantle, and Mr. L. F. Thomas (who were in the Department for the whole duration of the project), Mr. I. Leff, Mr. S. Andrzejewski, Mr. P. M. Foster, Mr. D. G. Mitchell (who were in the Department during part of the project); to members of the part-time teaching staff; and to the firms and students who use the Department's services, for the active and prolonged cooperation that made the work possible.

Mr. Hans Renold of International Business Machines, Ltd., and Dr. Mary Woodward, who directed the D.S.I.R. project at the South East Essex Technical College, both helped by apprais-ing an early draft, and by suggesting modifications for readers in the fields of industry and education.

The project would not have been initiated without the parti-cipation and advice of Dr. A. T. M. Wilson, Chairman of the Management Committee of the Tavistock Institute, who retained responsibility for the overall plan and took an active part at several important stages. We are also indebted to several of our other colleagues at the Tavistock Institute who gave help and advice. Mr. A. K. Rice read through the final drafts of this book and helped considerably with its structure and language. Our thanks are due to Miss Gillian Hayes-Newington, who acted as secretary to the project throughout, and to Miss Daphne Bostock who typed the final manuscript.

CHAPTER I

Technological Education and Managerial Studies

THE ROLE OF THE TECHNICAL COLLEGE

The two main kinds of educational institution catering for adolescents and young adults in Britain are universities and technical colleges. Universities are independent institutions, set up under Royal Charters or Acts of Parliament. They are self-governing communities. They have their own funds and have sufficient security to be able to resist direct pressures from external agencies whose convictions and prejudices could influence their teaching. Technical colleges are usually managed and financed by local education authorities under the regulations of the Ministry of Education, and hence cannot but be directly influenced by local and national policies. Under the terms of the Education Act, 1944, the council of each county is the local education authority of that county and, as such, is required to secure the provision for its area of adequate facilities for further education.[1]

Universities require concentration on academic study for at least three years (seldom with any official vacation experience in industry) and try to ensure that no other work interferes with academic concentration. Technical college courses, on the other hand, are usually interwoven with practical experience of one kind or another and most of them require only part-time attendance from students whose major commitment is full-time industrial employment. They prepare large numbers of young

[1] This is defined by the Act as 'full-time and part-time education for persons over compulsory school age and leisure-time occupation, in such organized cultural training and recreative activities as are suited to their requirements, for any persons over compulsory school age who are able and willing to profit by the facilities provided for that purpose.'

people for membership of professional institutions for which they will be eligible after completing both academic studies and a prescribed period of industrial experience. University education leads to the award of degrees. Technical college awards are usually certificates or diplomas. Where technical college courses lead to degrees, as they sometimes do, these are awarded by the universities who set and mark the examinations.

Technical colleges provide, inexpensively, to persons mostly in full- or nearly full-time employment, knowledge and skills capable of short-term practical application. Technical college education is less general and more advanced than school education and more applied, less theoretical, and less academically advanced than university education. There are, in all, about five hundred technical or commercial training establishments in England and Wales, varying from large colleges of technology, mainly in London and the county boroughs, to small technical institutes. There is some overlap between technical colleges and universities in the subjects taught and qualifications towards which students may work, but technical colleges cover a wider range of pure science, applied science, and other subjects than universities, include less advanced work within their courses, and cater widely for younger and part-time students. In each national age group there is a much higher proportion of technical college students than university students; there are, for instance, about four times as many students at age twenty, and ten times as many at age nineteen, registered at technical colleges as at universities.

The technical college lacks the prestige of the university within the educational and business worlds and in British life generally. It is nevertheless accepted as a valuable, even indispensable, social institution. Some people hold that the combination which the best technical colleges can provide of academic experience with parallel and concurrent experience in industry or commerce has advantages over a university education with subsequent entry into working life.

PHASES IN TECHNICAL AND SCIENTIFIC EDUCATION

The first important phase in technical and scientific education occurs in the secondary schools. There are three main types—

grammar, technical, and modern— taking about 20 per cent., 5 per cent., and 75 per cent. of each age group respectively. Technical schools provide a secondary education with an increasing technical bias in the later years of the course. It is not, of course, only or even mainly from technical schools that adult scientists and technicians are drawn. A very high proportion, perhaps a half, of boys in grammar and modern schools take science as their main subjects, and after leaving school a particularly high proportion of grammar school boys go on to study science at the universities.

After school an overlap exists between universities and technical colleges in the teaching of science and applied science subjects. Both train men for industry. It has long been the official view that universities and technical colleges must share responsibility for educating the future technical administrators and technically qualified managers of industry. In practice, however, society has looked mainly to the universities for the training of scientists, both for research and development, and of science teachers, and mainly to technical colleges for technical assistants and craftsmen.

Distinction is made between 'technologists' and 'technicians'. A recent Government White Paper on Technical Education described the technologist as one who had the qualifications and experience required for membership of a professional institution, and who had studied the fundamental principles of his chosen technology and should be able to use his knowledge and experience to initiate practical developments. Most university graduates in engineering and other applied sciences, and a good proportion of holders of Higher National Diplomas or Certificates, or similar qualifications, become technologists. A 'technician', on the other hand, was described as one qualified by specialist technical education and practical training to work under the general direction of a technologist. He required a good knowledge of mathematics and science related to his own speciality. Examples included assistant designers in factories and junior ranks of management on the shop floor.

[1] Ministry of Education, *Technical Education*. Cmd. 9703. Feb., 1956. London: H.M. Stationery Office.

EXPANSION IN TECHNOLOGICAL EDUCATION

Scientific and technical education has greatly expanded in Britain during the past two decades. The White Paper on Technical Education pointed out that 'Between 1938 and 1955 the number of university students in science and technology has doubled and since the Education Acts of 1944 and 1945, more schools and technical colleges have been built, more teachers have been recruited, and more interest has been shown in education by parents and employers than in any corresponding period in our history.' It goes on to stress that Britain is, nevertheless, in danger of being left behind by the immense efforts being made in the U.S.A., Russia, and Western Europe to train more scientific and technical manpower. 'One industry after another is being compelled to follow its competitor, supplier or customer in modernising its techniques, knowing that unless new materials are discovered and new methods applied, British industry may fall behind in the race. The pace of change is quickening, and with it both the need and the demand for technical education.' Within the definition of technical education the White Paper included not only the study of materials and mechanics, but also such subjects as economics, business management, wage systems, and human relations.

During the past five years the technical colleges have argued against what has seemed to them to be the policy of the present Government unduly to favour the universities through increased finances. They have argued that technical colleges already have many of the staff and facilities, including the contacts with industry, necessary for advanced technical education, and that universities, concentrating on the arts, pure science, and research, have limited enthusiasm for the training of technologists. Technical colleges have been reluctant to confine themselves to the training of technicians and craftsmen.

These comments were particularly stimulated during 1953 and 1954 when the Government showed its intention to enlarge and improve existing universities where science and technology already flourished, 'so that facilities for advanced technological education could be expanded with least loss of time and with the additional advantage of securing for the students all the benefits of sharing the corporate life of great universities'. In 1953 the Government announced an expansion of the Imperial

College of Science and Technology (University of London) at a cost of £14 million. The Chancellor of the Exchequer further announced in the House of Commons during 1954 that he had approved plans for further development of higher technological education at the universities of Glasgow, Manchester, Leeds, and Birmingham, with provision for later development at other universities.

Meanwhile, plans for technical colleges were under consideration. In mid 1955 the Minister of Education announced the projected establishment of a council responsible for making national awards in technology to students in technical colleges who successfully complete higher technological courses approved by the council. The diplomas would be designed to provide, at the first level, an educational qualification comparable in standard to a university degree. Early in 1956 far-reaching plans were announced for the further development of technical colleges. Building to the value of £70 million was proposed for England and Wales, to begin in the next five years, with the expenditure of a further £15 million on equipment.

The programme outlined in the White Paper was designed first to enable technical colleges in England and Wales to increase the number of advanced-course students from the present 9,500 a year to 15,000 as soon as possible, while adequately supporting them at lower levels; and second, to double the numbers of employed boys and girls under 18 (at present about 210,000) who are released for part-time day study. The Government favoured an increased use of sandwich courses for advanced technological students, lasting four or five years (with alternating periods of six months in college and industry). Those taking sandwich courses at the highest level would be eligible for the new award to be given by the National Council for Technological Awards.

TECHNOLOGICAL EDUCATION AND MANAGEMENT TRAINING

The Demand for Improved Management

The debate on the relative responsibilities of universities and technical colleges for technological education has been accompanied by concern that what has been learned at either should be applied. The demand is growing for men whose leadership abilities and managerial capacity matches their technological skill.

It has been demonstrated over and over again that a good technologist is not by virtue of his technological skill a good manager, nor a skilled craftsman necessarily a good foreman. These are 'under-developed' areas in the manning of industry.

The increasing 'rationalization' of private enterprise and the change from private to public companies and from family firms to firms run by paid managers is vitiating nepotism. When industry is changing rapidly men with the best managerial capacities are essential in key positions of responsibility. The growth of industrial complexity has made it essential that managers be able to integrate the contributions of technologists and other specialists and coordinate the work of teams. Also important in the development of management training has been the tendency for large industrial organizations to diversify their products and, complementarily, to decentralize their organization. In such circumstances, the manager working away from headquarters must absorb considerable general knowledge of the views and methods of the business as a whole and become closely identified with it, so that he is able more or less 'automatically' to reconcile the interests of his unit with those of the wider business. He must be able to interpret the actions of other managers within a shared basic outlook. Large organizations are beginning to accept that 'personnel controls' are at least as necessary, and can be as effective, as financial and administrative controls.

Managements seek increasingly to perpetuate their succession by programmes of development designed to ensure that selected persons of promise secure experience that will fit them for senior responsibilities as soon as the need and opportunity arise. It is now widely believed that it is economic to identify prospective top managers as early as possible and to give them as much experience as possible of different sides of business while they are still young. Such policies conserve the resources of business and help to attract and recruit an adequate level of staff. In today's sellers' market for labour the potential manager is free to chose the employer most likely to make full use of his talents.

At the level of first-line supervisors, men are also needed who can knit working groups into teams, retain their loyalty, and help them to identify with their tasks and with the concerns that employ them. Since the advent of full employment the day of the 'hire and fire' foreman has passed and with it the criterion of superior technical skill as the main or only qualification for positions of supervisory responsibility.

The Response of the Educational World

Educational institutions seem to agree only that standards of management should be improved and that technologists and technicians should have some form of training. They do not agree about how to train.

Some consider that a liberal education, or a wide treatment of pure science and technical subjects of the type received in most universities, in themselves comprise sufficient contribution to a man's capacity for leadership. In its comments on the Government White Paper on Technical Education, *The Times* wrote: '. . . for that special wisdom which the humanities can give there is perhaps more call than ever . . . there is work in the realm of politics, administration and management which can best be done by those trained in the liberal arts. It is true that they ought not in these days to be wholly ignorant of science, but those who aspire to handle men rather than machines will still be carried closest to the secret of it by the humanities.'[1]

This approach is challenged by the late Lord Cherwell's view that, 'Stimulating as some people find the verses of Catullus, reading them scarcely increases productivity.'[2] Official opinion seems influenced by both viewpoints. The White Paper stated that: 'A place must always be found in technical studies for liberal education. The time available often limits what can be done in the way of introducing into the curriculum subjects such as history, literature and the arts, but in any event a wide treatment of scientific and technical subjects is essential if students who are to occupy responsible positions in industry are to emerge from their education with a broad outlook.'

While it is sometimes disputed that special training in management is necessary for a liberally educated man, it is generally agreed that some form of training is necessary for some people. A distinction is often made between management training and education for management. The latter term refers to formal teaching which probably leads to a paper qualification and which may or may not contribute to the actual development of a

[1] *The Times*, 1st March, 1956.

[2] Quoted in editorial of *The Technical Journal*, 30th September, 1953.

manager. Management training is any organized or systematic programme of experience or teaching that is designed to instill or develop managerial competence.

On the whole, the universities have resisted appeals to include in their curricula such formal preparation for managerial responsibilities as management studies or similar forms of applied social science teaching. The nearest approaches have been the commerce degree courses given at several universities and the one-year courses in business administration at the London School of Economics. Arguments have been made from time to time in favour of the inclusion of management subjects towards the end of applied science degree courses.

University opinion seems to be that these subjects are not sufficiently 'mind-developing' and fundamental for first degree courses, and that the role of the university in preparing arts students for management roles is primarily to make them good citizens competent to appreciate the relation of industrial to other social institutions. University administrators have added that even within the commerce degree courses which come closest to management subjects they have enough to do in giving students a background knowledge of business subjects without adding 'management'. It is held to be necessary to defend the purity of the educational process from a destructive vocationalism and it is argued that management studies constitute a field of knowledge too new and too unorganized to be regarded as suitable for university curricula.

Opponents of these arguments point to existing vocational provision in universities for professions such as medicine, the law, architecture, engineering, agriculture, and teaching. They argue that the universities are still prejudiced against business as an occupation for educated people, and are still assuming that life can be divided into the same compartments as established university faculties. They point to accumulating knowledge about organizational behaviour, industrial sociology, and group psychology, and to the use made of these together with technical 'commerce' subjects in the business schools of American universities of high academic standing.

Opposition to management training in universities is not confined to the universities themselves. While many large businesses seek training for their rising managers, many individual businessmen have private reservations about what can be done by formal education. An authority on the subject has pointed out that it would derogate the pride of many a successful businessman in his own career if it were to be recognized that the ability to manage is not innate but may be assisted through intellectual preparation and special experience in early adult life.[1]

Much of the difficulty about the provision of managerial training in universities no doubt arises from the closeness of management to 'behaviour as a whole'. Many people seem to regard as an implicit insult the idea that they or their social equals should need training in management. It is apparently easier to accept the idea that management training is necessary for those without an academic background. A certain class bias affects the status of management studies. The fear also seems to exist that courses in management will hasten the era of 'the managerial society' in which experts on human behaviour will train students to manipulate others.

University studies that might contribute towards greater managerial efficiency have been further hindered by the bias of academic social science towards philosophy, laboratory experiments, and statistics. First-hand social research involving the observation and elucidation of ordinary day-to-day behaviour is fairly new in Britain; there does not exist in this country a mass of observations, insights, hypotheses comparable with that which sociologists and psychologists have built up about industry in the U.S.A. or which British anthropologists have built up about smaller non-industrial societies overseas.

While little formal management training has been undertaken by universities, it has developed rapidly at the technical colleges. For some years a demand has come from industrial employers seeking economical methods of improving the supervisory capacities of technicians and specialists with responsibility over others. It has also come from rising or ambitous young people seeking to improve their paper qualifications, from older men who feel held up in their careers, and even to some extent from university graduates who feel something lacking in their training and hope that the gap will be filled by applied study in a technical college.

Employers, as well as potential students, have influenced the increasing inclusion of 'management' subjects in several of the

[1] Urwick, L. F., Introduction to *Management Teaching*, p. viii., by Newman, Harry, and Sydney, D. M.

engineering, production engineering, and commerce courses given at technical colleges; in the curricula leading to formal qualifications in works management and foremanship, and in the inception, in 1946, of certificates and diplomas in management studies under the joint auspices of the British Institute of Management and the Ministry of Education.

Accordingly, formal training for management and supervsion is today concentrated in technical colleges. Although a few university graduates undertake such courses, the great majority of the students have no university education. The courses are generally attended either by students in technology, whose curricula for technological qualifications include one or two subjects like industrial administration, or by operatives, clerks, supervisors, technicians, and specialists seeking training in supervision or a paper qualification in management studies.

While technical colleges have a virtual monopoly of formal education for management or supervision, they are not the only bodies engaged in this work. Educational institutions in Britain have not been fully able to meet the need of British industry for senior management development. Firms wishing to provide for the future have had to send promising men overseas, or to the courses of such bodies as the British Institute of Management and the Industrial Welfare Society, or to the independent Administrative Staff College at Henley, or have had to devise internal courses and training schemes on their own or in collaboration with visiting consultants and other specialists. Many firms have their own training programmes for junior managers and supervisors, or enlist the aid of private and semi-private organizations. The technical colleges have, however, by far the largest share of the market of those attempting to improve their qualifications or competence in management and supervision; they are especially important as the main bodies to which people turn of their own accord for help.

Concurrently with the growth of interest in management studies, rapid development has occurred in the field today designated 'production engineering'. This has been associated especially with the stimulation of work study and work simplification during the war and subsequent export drive: large segments of British industry have sought greater productive efficiency in the short term by standardizing and reorganizing methods of work with existing equipment, and have used work study in designing incentive bonus schemes. Greater use has been made of systematic study and planning of machine design and layout and of the organization of work. Formal training schemes for production engineers were introduced in 1947 when the Higher National Certificates in Production Engineering were introduced by the Institutions of Mechanical and of Production Engineers. Special courses in work study are provided by technical colleges and by consulting firms.

Management and production engineering studies have much in common.[1] Both deal with administrative improvements, with a mixture of technological and social variables, and with ways of initiating productive changes in organizations. This has been recognized in the inclusion of certain required management subjects in courses leading to the qualifications of the Institution of Production Engineers. Furthermore, as in the case of management studies, the formal study of production engineering subjects has grown up almost entirely outside universities. Today very few university departments award degrees in production engineering (or its equivalent under some other title) while well over fifty technical colleges give classes in production engineering subjects.

[1] The combination of management studies and production engineering in one technical college department (such as exists at Acton) is rare. While it faces staff and students with the necessity of reconciling the viewpoints of engineers and social scientists it provides unusual opportunities for teaching and exploration concerning the situations involving both sociological and technical elements which make up the daily work of the industrial manager.

CHAPTER II

The Needs and Circumstances of Students

THE COLLEGE

Acton Technical College was situated, at the time of the project, just off Acton High Street. During the day its building also housed a secondary technical school. The College was the senior of nine technical colleges in Middlesex, and the only one that included full-time degree courses among its activities.[1] Its official catchment area contained a population of over one and a half million, of which the Borough of Acton contributed 15 per cent. The College was opened in 1928 to provide technical education to meet the rapid growth of population and industry in West Middlesex. At first the main load was essentially evening work, and full-time day courses were started in 1932. Annexes have had to be used and extensions built; the College had clearly outstripped its existing accommodation in an old-fashioned and noisy building, and new premises for the main departments were in the course of construction nearby.

The College contained six departments. As well as the Department of Management and Production Engineering there were departments of Chemistry and Biology, Mathematics and Physics, Mechanical Engineering, Electrical Engineering, and a combined Women's Department and Hotel Catering School. Each of these had a Head responsible for the organization and conduct of its work. The College had a full-time teaching staff of one hundred, supplemented by a part-time teaching staff of two hundred and fifty.

Grades of academic work ranged from teaching for charge-hands and apprentices to teaching for external university higher

[1] These led to degrees of the University of London.

degrees. There were nearly five thousand students; well over half of them were evening students, about a third part-time day students released from work by their employers, and about a tenth full-time day students.[1]

COURSES IN THE DEPARTMENT OF MANAGEMENT AND PRODUCTION ENGINEERING

At the time of study, the Department of Management and Production Engineering dealt with approximately three hundred students each year. Most of them were adults with industrial or commercial experience. The picture presented in this chapter applies particularly to the situation that existed during the first year of the project in the academic year 1954-5, when most of the intensive research with students took place. It therefore describes not the situation existing now, but the starting point of the changes described in later chapters. This study drew upon existing knowledge about students, and aimed to supplement it and extend its scope. In this way the wider pattern of the Department's place in students' careers could be seen more clearly.

The courses held in the Department during the academic session 1954-5 were either 'certificate' courses, which prepared students for examination for certain externally controlled certificates and diplomas, or 'college' courses, which were devised and controlled by the College itself. The courses and the distribution of students between them, are shown in *Table* 1.

[1] Since the end of the project, the College has been divided into a Regional College of Technology and a Local Technical College, now known as the Brunel College of Technology and the Acton Technical College. The Brunel College began teaching in September 1957, and is housed mainly in the new buildings. It contains the Department of Management and Production Engineering, and Departments of Chemistry, Physics, Mathematics, Electrical Engineering, Mechanical Engineering, and Electronics. It deals with teaching at the level of Higher National Certificates and above, and with the special adult courses of the Department of Management and Production Engineering. The Acton Technical College has a Science and Engineering Department and deals with teaching at the level of City and Guilds Certificates, Ordinary National Certificates, and the General Certificate of Education.

Table 1

DISTRIBUTION OF STUDENTS BETWEEN COURSES DURING 1954-5

Course	*No. of Students*	*Sub-totals*
1. *Management Certificate Courses*		
(a) Intermediate Certificate in Management Studies		
First year	28	
Second year	37	
Third year	28	
(b) Diploma in Management Studies		
First year	21	
Second year	12	
(c) Certificate in Foremanship and Works Supervision.	21	147
2. *Production Engineering Certificate Courses*		
(a) Higher National Certificate		
First year.	12	
Second year	17	
(b) Post-Higher National Certificate	68	97
3. *College Courses*		
(a) Methods Engineering (4 short day-time courses)	37	
(b) Methods Engineering (evening course)	18	
(c) Graduate Trainees	6	
(d) Entering Industry	6	67
Total		311

The Intermediate Certificate and the Diploma in Management Studies were awarded jointly by the British Institute of Management and the Ministry of Education. The courses leading to these qualifications dealt with various aspects of commercial and industrial management, organization, and history. Classes met in the evenings, twice or three times a week, and they attracted the largest group of students in the department.

The Certificate in Foremanship and Works Supervision was awarded by the Institute of Industrial Administration, and dealt with elementary works organization and labour management. The course took two years in most technical colleges, but only one at Acton. Classes met on two evenings each week. Holders of the certificate who wished to take the B.I.M. Certificate and Diploma were allowed to join the second year of the Intermediate Certificate course, augmenting the numbers joining that course from the first year. All these courses were curtailed or reorganized in later years.

Production engineering courses catered mainly for those seeking Associate Membership of the Institution of Production Engineers. Complete exemption from the examination requirements of the Institution was granted to holders of Higher National Certificates in Production Engineering, which bore certain endorsements obtained through further 'Post Higher National Certificate' study. The Certificates were awarded by the Institution of Mechanical Engineers and the Institution of Production Engineers. Certain of the Post Higher National Certificate subjects also satisfied the professional requirements of students in other Departments of the College, notably that of Mechanical Engineering, who joined these classes in considerable numbers. Classes met either on three evenings a week, or for one full day a week. A quarter of the production engineering students were released during the day by their employers for this purpose.

Among the College courses that on methods engineering dealt with work study techniques, their appraisal, and related personal and social issues. Four daytime courses were held during the 1954-5 session. They were of two kinds, extending over one month full time, or dividing the equivalent into full-time and part-time periods; there was, in addition, a part-time evening course. The graduate trainee course was instituted in the 1954-5 session. It consisted mainly of management studies and was run partly in collaboration with firms who sponsored the students and released them for one day per week. Members of the course were all graduates regarded by their employers as in training for managerial positions. The course for apprentices entitled 'Entering Industry' was another collaborative course instituted in the 1954-5 session. It was run as an experiment and involved a residential long weekend for the apprentices and a number of discussion meetings with the apprentices and their supervisors. There were a number of other short courses and meetings, the members of which were often drawn from courses mentioned above.

It is characteristic of technical college classes that their numbers rapidly diminish after the start of the course. The Acton Department was no exception. Of the 29 students who began the B.I.M. Certificate course in September 1954, 12 had left by the end of the session in June 1955. During the same period, 13 out of 21 first-year foremanship students and 3 out of 12 first-year production engineering students dropped out.

It was not possible to study the reasons for this dramatic wastage. Many students evidently change their minds about the worthwhileness of study, especially evening study, once they realize what incursions it makes into their time, and once they have had experience of attending a course and finding out what it is really like and what it entails for them.

STUDENTS IN THE DEPARTMENT

Most of what we have to say in this chapter about students applies to the certificate students in management and production engineering, particularly to those in the first year. These were the students with whom we had most contact, and who might be found in many other similar technical college departments. Some reference is made to the students on college courses who differed in many respects from the certificate students. It was in this field that the department made its major experiments and innovations.[1]

[1] Although we believe these students were not strikingly atypical, this chapter does not claim to discuss students of other subjects at a similar advanced level in Acton Technical College, or students in other colleges, adolescent students, or students of elementary or recreational subjects.

Age and Sex

Apart from the apprentices in the experimental 'Entering Industry' course, all students in the Department were adult and, with six exceptions, were men. They were in their middle and late twenties and early thirties. Ages varied between courses. The full-time methods engineering courses drew the most senior students, many being in their thirties and forties, and a few near retiring age. Evening students on courses in foremanship and works supervision tended to be rather older than other first-year evening students. Their average age was thirty, against twenty-six for both management and production engineering first-year students. The age range in the first year certificate students was from nineteen to fifty-three. Students in later years were correspondingly older.

Marital Status

Nearly all the foremanship students were married and were supporting their wives and children. In the other, younger, classes, a half or more were single, and often the wives of the married ones went out to work.

Occupations

The occupations of students in the Department are shown in *Table* 2, together with the courses they were following.

In the classification of jobs adopted in the table, 'manager' refers to someone holding a position at least at the level of, say, Area Sales Manager, Assistant Production Manager, or Office Manager. A 'specialist' is, for instance, a qualified chemist, accountant, surveyor, or copywriter. 'Representatives' include technical sales representatives. 'Supervisors' include foremen, chargehands and those in supervisory roles in offices and special departments. A 'junior technician' is a draughtsman or improver, an inspector, laboratory assistant, or work study assistant. 'Clerks' include special clerical grades such as statistical, costing, and pay clerks. 'Operators' may be highly skilled or unskilled, and include storemen, fitters, mechanics, drivers, and toolmakers. 'Trainees' may be management trainees, graduate apprentices, or technical trainees of various kinds. These categories are not easy to apply in some cases where the name of the job is known

Table 2 DISTRIBUTION OF STUDENTS BY COURSE AND OCCUPATION, 1954-5 SESSION

	OCCUPATION									
COURSE	*Managers*	*Specialists*	*Representatives and Buyers*	*Supervisors*	*Junior Technicians*	*Clerks*	*Operators*	*Trainees*	*Unknown or None*	*TOTAL*
B.I.M. Intermediate Certificate										
1st year	6	3	4		7	3	1	3	1	28
2nd year	4	4	3	8	8	7		3		37
3rd year	6	5	8	1	3	4	1			28
B.I.M. Diploma										
1st year	5	5	2	2	3	3		1		21
2nd year	3	1	1	2	3	2				12
Certificate in Foremanship				8		10	3			21
Sub-total Management students	24	18	18	21	24	29	5	7	1	147
Production Engineering										
H.N.C. 1st year					8		3	1		12
H.N.C. 2nd year					16			1		17
Post-H.N.C.	4	25	2	1	24		2	10		68
Sub-total Production Engineering students	4	25	2	1	48	0	5	12	0	97
Methods Engineering										
Day	4	8		12	7	2		3	1	37
Evening	1	4		1	11			1		18
Graduate Trainees								6		6
Entering Industry								6		6
Sub-total College students	5	12	0	13	18	2	0	16	1	67
Total	33	55	20	35	90	31	10	35	2	311

but the actual work and responsibility involved are not known, for instance, at the borderline between junior technician and qualified specialist.

As can be seen from the table, students on the British Institute of Management courses came from an especially wide variety of occupations. The majority held fairly junior positions in manufacturing industry, though some worked in commercial, transport, public or military undertakings. The specialists, junior technicians, and clerks numbered half of the total. These included draughtsmen, ratefixers, work study officers, engineers, statisticians, and planning and costing clerks.

Most of the students in the foremanship course were already in supervisory positions or were doing some kind of special clerical work such as estimating, planning, and costing. Specialists and technicians predominated among the production engineering students.

The methods engineering day students were usually managers, specialists, and technicians, many of them being already engaged in work study. One complete course was given to maintenance workshop foremen. Generally speaking, the methods engineering students held more senior positions than those in certificate courses. Evening methods engineering students were nearly all specialists and technicians.

Education

There are three main routes in Britain for those seeking careers in industry. A large proportion of grammar school pupils take science subjects and some, joined by public schoolboys, go up to university to take what we shall call a 'technical' qualification. The second route takes people through public and grammar schools to a 'non-technical' degree. The third takes people through the technical and secondary modern schools, or less often through grammar schools, and from there through technical colleges to National and Higher National Certificates. This third route, like the first, may be technical. The division between technical and non-technical is made for our present purpose and is somewhat arbitrary. A 'non-technical' subject is not necessarily an arts subject, but one whose procedure or techniques are not likely to be applied directly in industry. Technical qualifications can lead to general management by way of senior specialist posts with little direct managerial responsibility, or through production management. Non-technical qualifications make both these fields difficult to enter, disposing the holder rather to commercial or marketing routes to management.

The educational backgrounds of the students were closely linked with the routes they were following in their careers and with their current posts.

The first-year B.I.M. Intermediate class course exemplifies this. Six out of twenty-eight had technical degrees. They had come up via grammar school and university and were working in production management or in technical specialist jobs like engineering research. One had a non-technical degree via a grammar school, and worked as the personal assistant to a director of a large firm. Eight more had followed the academic path as far as the grammar school, and Higher or General School Certificates. Their jobs were widely varied—junior manager, time study engineer, buyer, representative, labour planning trainee. Two others had followed the technical certificate route, one successfully, being a graduate trainee, and the other, who failed his Higher National Certificate, being a time study engineer. Most of the rest, with no major certificates or qualifications, had been to secondary modern schools, and had a wide variety of jobs of a rather lower level than those from grammar schools, including clerks and operatives. In the later years of the B.I.M. courses, the proportion of technical graduates or those with equivalent qualifications was as high as in the first year.

Of the foremanship students most had attended secondary modern schools. A quarter had attended grammar schools. A few had previously taken other sorts of part-time certificate. mostly directly relevant to the technical content of their jobs.

Production engineering students were *ipso facto* following the third of the educational routes we have described—the technical certificate route. Rather more came from grammar schools than from modern or technical schools, though all three types of school and their equivalents were well represented. Proportions varied from year to year. Classes in each year of the course contained one or two students who had already obtained in another field qualifications that might be considered higher than that for which they were studying; for instance the graduate trainees, or holders of the mechanical engineering Higher National Certificate following the equivalent production engineering course, or people who had already achieved membership of other professional institutions taking endorsement subjects in part qualification for membership of the Institution of Production Engineers.

Complete records are not available of the educational backgrounds of the methods engineering students taking the one-month full-time course during the 1954-5 session, though it is known that twelve out of the thirty-seven were graduates or their equivalents.

Firms Employing Students

Students worked in a large number of firms. More than one hundred firms were represented, including most of the large firms in or near Acton. Three-quarters of those firms were represented by only one student. In the preceding year, 1953-4, the proportion was the same, but many of the firms were different. As only a handful of these firms were supporting the attendance of their employees, there was thus a substantial proportion of students coming on their own, unsupported by their firm financially or by recent tradition and example within the firm.

A handful of large firms had a dozen or score of their employees attending, whether this was known to them or not. The same firms were represented from year to year in the 'top ten', and these same firms were familiar to other departments in the College. They supplied governors as well as students. In all, nearly half of the students in the Department came from the 'top ten' firms. It was not merely their size that gave these firms such a large representation. A student coming from them was likely to know others in the firm who were attending, or who had attended, this or some other college.

Intellectual Capacities

Several classes of management and production engineering students completed written intelligence tests designed to indicate differences in general intellectual capacity. The tests chosen for the battery were the Mill Hill Vocabulary Test, a Verbal Intelligence Test, and a Reasoning Test. These three tests were standardized against a large army population in war-time whose scores may be taken, without serious error, to represent the general population. The tests are known to be good measures of 'general intelligence', i.e. the general, all-round capacity for carrying out activities that involve seeing relations, 'grasping the point', being able to marshal information and produce new arrangements of it.

The great majority of students returned scores higher than those expected from 90 per cent of the general population. This suggests that, in intellectual capacity, students in the Department were roughly equivalent to a university undergraduate population, and to the general run of applicants for management traineeships in large firms to which the Tavistock Institute has access by reason of its consultant services in this field. There were hardly any students in the senior years of the long courses who were not within the top 10 per cent of the population and higher scores were returned by more of them than by students in earlier years. This would suggest that it was increasingly difficult for a student to survive until the later years of courses of the standard given in the Department unless he was in the most intelligent 10 per cent of the population. There seemed to be no difference between the management courses and the Higher National Certificate courses in this respect.

The picture of the student population is thus of wide diversity in age, educational level, and job, though less in intelligence. Very many of the students were in some kind of technical specialist industrial employment, these forming the majority of the production engineering certificate students, who, by and large, work in fairly junior positions. Clerks and foremen tended to fill the foremanship course, while the evening management courses attracted an enormous variety of students. One group appearing regularly among the management students were the qualified technical specialists, usually engineers, more of whom had come up via the academic path than by the technical certificate path. More homogeneous groups were attracted by the 'College' courses, for instance work study specialists and works managers to the methods engineering courses, and graduate trainees and apprentices to their particular courses.

CONDITIONS OF STUDY

Reaching the College

Students took a lot of trouble to get to the College because of the wide area over which their homes and work places were spread. Home addresses of students were spread over most of Middlesex, West London, and beyond, ranging from Gerrards Cross to Molesey, and Maidenhead to Central London,[1] and including over eighty separate postal areas. The area was fairly regularly covered as far as the outer London 'dormitory' suburbs, and then reached out along the main railways and roads. Sometimes, if either place of work or home area was far from the College, the other would be fairly near, but it was by no means the rule that students either worked or lived locally. Few boroughs or districts supplied more than a handful of students and these 'favourite' areas were nearly all within five miles of Acton, and mostly in Middlesex, though a couple of London boroughs near by provided as many students as most neighbouring Middlesex boroughs. The five-mile westward radius includes the edge of the substantially built-up residential and industrial western suburbs of Greater London and extends into the newer and more residential outer suburbs.

The areas in which people worked were less regularly dispersed than were home areas, although they were spread as wide. The tendency of the Management Department of Acton to attract 'local' students is most apparent in the distribution of work areas, due largely to the fact that some of the 'top ten' firms were actually in Acton.

There was a slight tendency to attract students who lived near by, and a stronger tendency to attract students who worked in a few big firms near by. There were several other technical colleges in the 'core' of the catchment area offering some or all of the same courses as did Acton.

This wide geographical distribution of students involved students in considerable travelling. A first-year evening student

[1] Residents of Middlesex are entitled to enrol in any Middlesex college, and are not confined to the nearest college that provides the particular course they want. Residents of neighbouring counties are charged higher fees, known as 'out-county' fees. Often two counties will make a reciprocal arrangement under which each admits students from the other at the normal fee. Middlesex and London do this. Other county councils will pay out-county fees incurred by their own residents.

for instance, was likely to spend, on the average, about half an hour in travelling from home to work, and in travelling to the College from either home or work, whichever it might be. He might have spent as little as five minutes or as much as an hour and a half on each of these journeys. He usually came direct from work to College, and if he did, he was unlikely to have eaten anything before lectures. In all, those who could get a meal before lectures numbered less than two-fifths of the total. Nearly a half expected no food.

This was vividly brought home to us one evening, when, at the end of a questionnaire one class was completing for us, most of them rushed out immediately. 'Look here,' said one, 'some of us haven't eaten since 12, and this is our only chance to get something.' 'Something' was a cup of tea and a cake, provided by the caretaker of the school building near the College, in which the class was held.

Many students used their own transport. A half of the first-year students always relied on walking or public transport, but the others sometimes used their own transport, most of them running motor cycles or cars. Those in the B.I.M. and foremanship evening classes had little difficulty over parking, as these classes were held in the school building not far from the College, whose playground could be used for this purpose. Others were less lucky for there was little parking space in or near the College.

Physical Conditions in the College

Students in those classes conducted in the neighbouring school had to sit at children's desks in rooms displaying, for instance, specimens of growing beans and informative posters about the peoples of the world. Even in the main building of the College, which was shared with a junior technical school, and was in fact designed as one, rooms had often to be used which were similarly appointed. These conditions were commented upon by students in discussion and interview, and served to heighten existing feelings about returning to school. Whether these comments indicated only feelings of resentment at being treated as children or were sometimes tinged with relief at being allowed to return to a dependent role, the surroundings did not contribute to the dignity of the class or of the subjects studied.

Students were, therefore, working under adverse physical conditions, travelling several miles after a full day's work, and sitting, often hungry, in desks designed for children half their size. Except for ten or twenty minutes' break for tea the classes lasted three hours.

Individual Study

In addition to their attendance at College, students were assigned reading, essays, and exercises to carry out at other times. Students, staff, and the authorities called this 'homework', a name that emphasized the school-like aspects of the College atmosphere. Most students spent three or four hours each week in work outside class periods, individual estimates varying from hardly anything up to twelve hours. Production engineering students tended to spend longer than management students. Students were asked, at the beginning of the first year, how long they expected to spend on homework. After a few months they found themselves spending half as long as they originally estimated. These early estimates, made without the knowledge of what would be demanded, can be seen as part of the 'price' the students were at first prepared to offer to the College for what they hoped they would receive in return. They reflected the students' early valuation of the course and their expectation of the demands to be made on them.

Very few students preferred to work in libraries or at work rather than at home. Most of those who worked at home said that they had suitable rooms, but the younger married students, in particular, tended to live under crowded conditions and found study at home difficult. Several mentioned the effects of their work on others in the house, such as friction over mealtimes, and demands on others for quiet.

Effects on Home Life

Attendance at the College, and work for their courses, affected the home lives of students, if only in the substitution of this activity for others. Before they began their courses, most expected to lose at least some leisure time. The very few who did not expect to lose leisure time either did not count this as a significant effect upon their 'home lives and other activities', or made course-going a major activity in their lives which did not 'interfere' with other activities. A few students expected to have to curtail some hobbies and other activities, to have less opportunity for seeing their families, working around the house, or helping with the children. As the course progressed, they discovered that they had to sacrifice more activities than they anticipated. It was not only those who expected considerable sacrifices who stayed the course; some left who did not expect sacrifices, but some left who did.

Courses seemed to demand more of students than they first thought. They found that to use even half the time they had planned to spend on study meant more sacrifices than they expected. Their appreciation of what might be involved was not realistic. Also we shall see how students found that the returns from their courses were not always what they had hoped.

Help from Employers

The extent to which students enjoyed the support and help of their employers varied widely. Members of the College's own courses for methods engineers, graduate trainees, and apprentices were all nominated by their firms, who paid the College fees and sent them to the College in the firm's time. Even so, the students did not always feel that the interest their employers were taking in them was entirely positive; usually it was—the student being groomed for a new post, or sent to improve his skill in a new speciality. Sometimes a student was sent to the College because the course or the subject was under scrutiny; a senior manager came to a methods engineering course, for instance, to see whether this subject might be of use to his firm. While it is usually regarded as a compliment for an employee to be chosen by his firm for training, students sometimes felt that being sent on a course meant that they were being criticized for a deficiency in their ability or training rather than that the firm was recognizing their potential. A few felt that they were being 'got out of the way' for a while.

In spite of occasional doubts by students, the College courses, especially those designed in collaboration with firms, appeared to differ greatly from other courses because of the students' enjoyment of the support of their employers. This enhanced the importance of the course, and made attendance in some way a shared enterprise between their employers and themselves. Of students on the management or production engineering certificate courses, only a few received such serious support. About half received no kind of support or help whatever.

Most of the help amounted to being allowed to leave work early on class nights or being given paid leave before or during examinations. Support sometimes came from a general policy of encouraging part-time education in the firms, particularly in the few firms that provided most of the Department's students. The importance of general policy as well as the sympathy of immediate superiors was illustrated by the experience of one student whose employers were indifferent to his attendance until there was a change in high-level policy that led to their warmly supporting him. A student in such a firm might have seen courses advertised in the firm, or know people who had attended courses. Personnel or training officers might recommend courses, or the firm might agree to pay or refund fees and the cost of books for approved courses.

Only one in six of the certificate students was, however, having his fees paid. A recommendation to a course or an agreement to give financial help did not necessarily imply that employers were seriously supporting a particular individual or were expecting very much from him. Nor was a student who was paying his own fees necessarily being ignored by his firm. This makes it difficult to say exactly what the support of employers really amounted to, but it seems that part-time certificate students were not, as a rule, receiving serious individual backing. They had an even chance of getting general support because of the general educational policy of their firms, or of being granted minor local concessions in working hours by their immediate superiors.

STUDENTS' VIEWS

Expectations

Important differences between students on the College courses and those on the certificate courses become apparent when the students' expectations of courses and their reactions to them are examined.

Members of the College courses joined primarily because they were instructed to to so by their employers. Whatever the students' reactions to this, and, to a considerable extent, whatever the firm's intentions, the subject matter of the course was assumed to be directly relevant to the work the student was doing or was soon to be doing. Students expected to learn about the Acton approach to work study, or to be taught to use techniques in work study. They judged courses according to these shorter-term criteria, rather than against expectations of 'getting on' or becoming a 'manager'. This is not to say that students' expectations about these courses fitted exactly with what the courses actually were, or that expectations other than the main one did not need to be recognized and handled by the Department. With new courses, in particular, the expectations of both staff and students were less well defined, and considerable experimenting was sometimes needed.

Certificate students saw their courses as in some way a contribution to their personal advancement. Of course, students usually had several reasons for coming—some immediate, some more long term, some realistic and some less so. When asked simply what had made them decide to come, most students mentioned personal advancement or some intermediate goal that would contribute to it. The predominance of the career aim was made very clear when nearly every new student said he expected his studies to lead him to a better job. More expected to get better jobs with employers other than their own, especially among the management students.[1] Foremanship students tended in the other direction.

Differences in approaches to courses were reflected in the way students heard about their courses. Production engineering students wishing to take examinations had necessarily already completed an Ordinary National Certificate at Acton or another technical college and knew about the existence of the Higher National Certificate. They would ask where such a course might be followed, or were told of this one within their firms or by

[1] This is interesting for two reasons. First, it suggests that students felt their current employers did not appreciate them. Secondly, it suggests one reason why some employers are uneasy about their staff going to courses—a feeling that this might encourage them to leave for other posts.

friends. The subject matter of the courses usually had some connection with their work, as can be seen from the predominance among them of such technical and specialist personnel as time study engineers, draughtsmen, and jig and tool designers. Management students tended to have heard of the courses through a wider range of channels, through friends, through an initial rather vague, inquiry of their own, or through someone in their firms.

Attitudes towards Training and Formal Qualifications

There were differences between classes in the emphasis placed on the value of the qualifications being sought and on the importance of shorter-term goals.

The foremanship students linked their courses with their present jobs more than did the other students. They tended to expect better jobs with their own employers, rather than with others, and were more inclined to talk about the value of the course in relation to their present jobs. Some were coming explicitly to learn about the practices of other firms, so that they might evaluate their own firms' methods and training schemes. This was occasionally a somewhat clandestine activity as far as the support and knowledge of their employers were concerned. Others were preparing themselves for possible promotion. One said he always prepared himself for the next job up, and set himself an ambition. Usually the students' attendance was self-initiated and self-supported.

The production engineering students were almost unanimous that the Higher National Certificate in Production Engineering was their minimum qualification for better jobs, though many of them felt that the H.N.C. in Mechanical Engineering might really be better for them. There were various reasons for this. Most suspected that the holder of a 'mechanical certificate' as it was often called, derived a higher status from his qualification than did the holder of a 'production certificate'. Some felt that it was actually a better qualification for the content of their work, even for production engineers. Others, particularly those who were not designers, thought that the mechanical certificate was too theoretical for a production man, but better for a designer. There were yet others, including designers, who thought it did not matter for the work itself which certificate was held.

Doubts about the comparative value of the production engineering certificate were linked with frequent feelings that the mechanical certificate was too mathematical, and too 'hard'. If a student felt this, then mechanical certificate holders might well, in his eyes, enjoy a superior status, in addition to whatever difference there might be in others' eyes. He might, alternatively, devalue the mechanical certificate saying, in effect, 'I don't want it anyway—I'm a practical man.' Or he might refuse to see any difference, 'Either certificate is as good as the other.' We cannot say which of these expressed viewpoints is objectively accurate. What is important is the concern of the students in these arguments, which could derive from feeling that they were not clever enough for the mechanical certificate as well as from the objective accuracy of the arguments.

There was another source of doubt and disagreement for the production students. Some felt that the production certificate syllabus was too wide and consequently too general, while others felt this was proper for a general qualification. They were aware here of a conflict between a desire for a certificate as a general qualification to help them in competition for jobs, and a desire for detailed study of particular subjects to help them in their own daily work.

Management certificate students were less impressed than the production engineering students with the value of the diploma they sought. In discussion, they tended to ask what was the general opinion of the diploma in industry, rather than to say what they thought it was. One senior student said that the course had to be sold to industry through the subsequent success of people who had taken it. Both senior and new students realized that few, if any, of their own superiors possessed the diploma or anything like it. There was a correspondingly greater interest in the value of the content of the course. Management students tended to emphasize that the knowledge was important. Many, though, were quite vague when they came about exactly how the certificate or course could or would help them.

Ambitions

The conscious ambitions of students were fairly consistent between courses. The typical picture that a new student held of his destination was that of a departmental, production, or possibly works manager, or a specialist production engineer, in a salary range of £1,000 to £1,500 per annum. Some had more limited ambitions. One said he did not set himself any particular ambition, but wanted to ensure himself a comfortable life, and to do a bit better than his parents did. He set his goal as a nice house with a radio and television; the height of luxury would be to run his own car. Most were less modest—we have seen that many already had cars—but there were few who set themselves really high ambitions: 'I don't think I'll ever get to director level, because you need social connections for that. Somebody who is likely to finish up at that level would not have come from a technical college, but would have taken a Cambridge degree.'

We know that senior students sometimes held quite responsible posts already, but we have less information about their aspirations. It was possible to see some differences in purpose among the senior management students that probably existed among students in earlier years of the course, though they were less easy to see; they are related to education. One kind of management student was working his way up the promotion ladder, lacking major education qualifications, and using the diploma to help him meet this lack. Of those with degrees or equivalent qualifications, some, the followers of the 'academic' or non-technical educational route, wanted to supplement their general education with studies more closely related to actual industrial practice. A third group, fairly well defined, though not large, consisted of the graduate engineers we have mentioned before. They said they wanted to add to their special and local knowledge of industry a wider knowledge of the other aspects of organization, either to see better where they fitted in, or to help them take on more management responsibility as they were promoted. They tended to stay the course, and teachers sometimes remarked that the engineers were particularly rewarding to teach.

Reactions to Classes

In their first year, management students took two subjects, one dealing with a general introduction to management roles and structures and practices, and the other dealing with industrial and economic history. Even before any lectures in either they expected the first to be helpful and the second not, while expecting to like them equally. Later, their preference was confirmed and sharpened and they came strongly to prefer the lectures on 'Nature of Management'.

There was a parallel in the foremanship class, where lectures in industrial history were expected and found to be less likeable or helpful than lectures in production, planning, costing, etc. In our field studies of firms which formed part of the project, we found again clearly that it was subjects like these that foremen and supervisors thought would be helpful. The preference in these classes for the more obviously and immediately relevant subjects shows that however long-term their aim in coming, students wanted something immediately valuable if their interest was to be maintained. They were impatient to get at what they saw as the heart of the matter and to avoid subjects of a more general educational nature. These seemed to them to be more like school subjects, and although several students said in interview that they wanted to fill in gaps that they felt existed in their general education, they seemed sensitive when a lecturer did just this.

Production engineering students seemed to have less of this impatience; this may well be related to their more homogeneous educational backgrounds. They did not have such high hopes of liking any of their subjects, and later had more mixed, though generally more favourable, impressions of what they were getting.

Relations between Students

Students did not, on the whole, expect to find discussions with fellow students very helpful to learning, and in fact each student's contact with the others was minimal. Hardly any friendships were developed within the classes and very little discussion of course material took place spontaneously. Towards the end of the first term, one of the management students described how the members of the class were beginning to nod towards each other and to move around freely at the tea break. At the end of the evening everybody went home—they were tired and hungry. This seemed to be a general pattern.

Whereas it is often said, and was said by these students, that one of the valuable features of courses run outside an individual firm was that an interchange of opinion was made possible, the students in fact made little explicit use of this themselves. They cannot be said to have formed themselves into a temporary community as full-time technical college and, particularly, university students tend to. This applies with somewhat less force to senior classes, which consisted of a small band of survivors of a five-year marathon.

Attitudes to Departmental Methods

The teaching methods that students preferred were class discussions with lecturers, practical demonstrations by lecturers, and formal lectures. In particular, the management students wanted 'practical demonstrations by lecturers'. There were mixed feelings about formal lectures. Some wanted them and liked them ('They sit there waiting to be lectured at,' said one lecturer), whereas others pointedly disliked them.

Students' reactions to their lecturers and the Department in general were hypercritical. Any instance of unpunctuality, lack of preparation, apparent lack of interest, overlapping beween lectures, and administrative slips were subject to repeated complaint, freely expressed to us, though not at first to the Department. Management students in particular expected high standards of teaching and a high standard of demonstration of good management from the Department. They felt that if their teachers did not manage their own organization well, they would be unlikely to be able to teach good management to others.

THREE STUDENT PROFILES

We can begin to draw together some of the themes running through all this material by looking at a few brief individual cases. No student was typical of the Department, nor did the students fall neatly into types, although some distinctions and divisions have been made for clarity while discussing particular areas of interest. Thus, any attempt to summarize this mass of varied information must falsify it to some extent for any one student. The individuals described here are chosen to illustrate the diversity as well as some of the consistencies among the students.

A Foremanship Student

One student, whom we shall call Mr. Brook, worked as a foreman in a wiring department of a radio firm. He was thirty-one years old when interviewed, and was married with two children.

He was born in the country not far from London but the family moved several times during his childhood. His father worked in the fruit and vegetable trade, either as a representative for larger firms or, for limited periods, in business on his own.

Mr. Brook attended local elementary schools (now 'primary' and 'secondary modern'), and he won a scholarship to a London secondary school, but was prevented from taking it up by a family move. He changed jobs several times after leaving school, finding none of them very satisfactory until he took one in a radio firm. He picked up knowledge of radio and electricity and was soon made a chargehand.

Further changes of job were interrupted by R.A.F. service, during which he was an N.C.O. in the equipment section. On his release he found his way to more specialized radio work, and greater responsibility, but had reached something of a barrier.

He took the foremanship course at Acton, on the advice of his firm's education officer, to help improve what he felt was a deficient general education. He stayed the course, passed the examination, and decided to go on to the B.I.M. Intermediate and Diploma, in a different college. He regarded himself as a practical man, and in fact had built his own house and some of its contents. He and his wife liked to fill their spare time with practical pursuits, though during the year of the course he seemed to enjoy relaxing more than he did before. He aimed for a job as a works manager or something like it, which seemed preferable to personnel work. He would have liked his own radio-parts business, but felt that the larger firms had really captured the market, and that his best prospects lay with them.

A Production Engineering Student

A second student, called here Mr. Page, was taking the Higher National Certificate in Production Engineering. He was twenty-seven years old, married and employed as a draughtsman in an electrical equipment firm. He was born on a farm where his father was an estate worker. When Mr. Page was ten, his father, like many others, lost his farm job, and went to work in an engineering factory. Mr. Page left school at fourteen, primarily to augment the family's income, and because he felt that he was learning little of use. He had, too, more practical inclinations, and found work as a laboratory boy in a steel works. where, two years later, he was apprenticed in the drawing office.

During the five years of his apprenticeship he attended local schools and colleges at night or during the day and studied for his Ordinary National Certificate, which he did not complete, through failing in single subjects. At the end of his apprenticeship he changed his job and became a jig and tool designer in an electronic instrument firm. Continuing his part-time studies, he completed his Ordinary National Certificate and went on to the Higher Certificate, meanwhile joining his present firm. His studies were interrupted when the firm moved to London, and again during the following year when there was a rush of work in his office. He decided to try again at Acton.

During his first year at Acton he moved into his house and his wife had their first child. At work, he was the senior of the three draughtsmen in his office. He liked his job, was satisfied with his salary (which rose from £750 to £825 per annum soon after the interviews), and got on well enough with his boss, the chief designer engineer. He had no immediate prospect of promotion, but did not intend to leave. He was not, therefore, seeking the H.N.C. for prospective immediate gain. He felt that if he passed this examination he would go on to complete the Higher National Certificate, but if he failed, he would not try again. In the event he passed not only the first, but also the second-year examinations, thus completing his Higher National Certificate.

A Management Student

The last of our three individual sketches is of a student in the first year B.I.M. Intermediate Certificate class. 'Mr. Ford', aged twenty-eight, was assistant supply manager of an engineering manufacturing firm. He was married, without children. His father was the advertising manager of a group of local newspapers.

Mr. Ford attended a grammar school, and entered London University to take a mathematics degree. He failed some of his sessional examinations, through what he felt was lack of work, and was called up. He spent two years in the army, during which he reached the rank of staff sergeant. When he was released he spent a short time working as an assistant and prospective partner with a man running his own small craft business, but soon left to join his present firm as an order clerk. In six years he worked his way to be the assistant supply manager. He had been given special tasks, notably the reorganization of a supply department in one of the company's provincial branches, and the training of a manager for that department. He felt that there was little chance of promotion in his own department but he did not want to move into the sales department where there was a better chance of promotion and increased pay. His present job earned him £650 a year, with a possible ceiling of £1000.

Mr. Ford's wife worked full-time as a secretary in his own firm. His main spare-time activity was his membership of the local Round Table (similar to Rotary Club). It was not the prospect of gaining a certificate that brought him to the College, but a wish to learn about management. He hoped this would bring his a better job with his own employers—or others. During the first year of the course he felt that he was indeed learning principles and practices that were of value in his own job. He finished his course, passed the examination, and went on to the second-year course, which, we subsequently learned, he completed successfully.

DIVERSITY OF AIMS, NEEDS, AND PROSPECTS

Certain recurrent themes may now be summarized. Students sent by their employers to the courses devised and controlled by the College itself were rather different in their approach from the students on the part-time certificate courses. The certificate students were more concerned with long-term aims and the achievement of ambitions that were by no means high. Students, by and large, saw themselves heading for junior management or a little above. Foremanship students were the oldest, and perhaps the least ambitious. They were rather more concerned with the immediate applicability of what they were learning. Production engineering students were clearer in their aims, and perhaps less critical of their courses. Management students were the most vague in their aims, and in their reasons for coming, and were more critical of their courses.

When we remember that many students, particularly in evening management certificate courses, leave during their first year, we can begin to see a caricature of the unsuccessful student. He is a junior industrial employee, lacking in major educational qualifications, aspiring vaguely and modestly towards management positions. He comes to take a certificate in management, hoping it will lift him somehow over the barriers he is otherwise unable to climb. Or perhaps he attempts to emulate the success of superiors by dogged years of study for what seems to him the least difficult and most practical higher engineering qualification he can find. He is impatient, hypercritical, dependent, and sensitive when at College, showing qualities that hardly demonstrate his capacity to manage. He becomes disappointed and drifts away.

The College often seems to be used as a second chance—a new opportunity for a student to evaluate himself and his prospects. The College is almost like an extra appeal system for such students. Many students using it in this way will be disillusioned; the 'second chance' they need lies deeper and earlier in their lives, and has less to do with adult education than with personal adjustment. Others will find their new chance enough.

Of those who leave, not all are disillusioned drifters. Some students look around them and see how their own superiors have achieved their positions and wonder whether the efforts they are making are really worth while. Perhaps they will win promotion without a certificate—particularly in management, though less so in production engineering. Thrusters as well as drifters leave their course before the end.

What of those who stay—are they likely to win promotion to senior positions? Certainly they are intelligent enough, and some already do hold responsible positions. Many of the production engineering students who keep up the work are progressing as fast as their educational route allows them to. It is the well-tried and respected 'hard way', and determination is needed for a student to overcome successive educational barriers, and to set his goals considerably higher than those his family have achieved. On the management courses there are people aiming to increase their appreciation of aspects of industry that they have had no previous opportunity of studying or knowing, so that they will be better equipped to take wider responsibility.

Students seem to have a clearer idea of their capacities and aims by the time they have spent several years on a course. They lose some of their illusions. Those with more solid achievement behind them seem to stay the courses better and, during the management courses in particular, some students are able to derive enough to help them expand their appreciation and understanding of industrial situations. It cannot be said of the senior management students as much as of some of the new ones that they want a certificate in management to make up for a deficiency in capacity to manage: yet without such study many men of similar background, age, and intelligence have achieved higher positions or seem likely to. It does not look, as yet, as though production engineering courses are as attractive to promising young engineers as some other ways of qualifying. Similarly, it does not look as though long management courses are, at present, the source of many developing managers.

The Department cannot, by itself, turn a student into a manager or a competent production engineer or specialist. Yet if it should accept into a course a person who is unlikely to become one, but seeks a certificate in order to 'get on', then that person is bound to meet disillusionment and disappointment, because he wants more help than any certificate course can give him. Any student needs more than just a course or certificate, and experiences some disappointment and resentment during his attendance if he is not getting it. Some derive enough help from their courses to stay them out, and make use of what they learn.

CHAPTER III

Circumstances and Attitudes of Local Firms

Many firms are concentrated near Acton Technical College. They vary in size, products, and manufacturing processes, and range from some of the largest food manufacturing and engineering factories in Britain to comparatively small firms acting as independent machine-shops for their larger neighbours.

The viewpoints and practices of these firms in training for management and production engineering were clearly important for the College. Exploratory interviews were accordingly conducted with nine local firms, three of which were selected for further detailed work. In this way the comments of senior managers in exploratory interviews could be supplemented by production managers and junior supervisory staff. We could also make independent observations. One other firm allowed us to observe one of their internal training courses, which we discuss in Chapter VI.

TRAINING AS AN INDUSTRIAL ACTIVITY

For the firms, education and training were means to ends. Training was subordinate to making profit, and managements attached limited importance to it. It was usually located within the personnel department. The personnel manager was not usually on the company board. Personnel and training functions were clearly regarded as subordinate to sales, production, and finance, most of which were headed by directors. To the extent that senior managements were convinced that investment in training would contribute towards their overall economic purpose, they were prepared to make such an investment. Beyond this they were sometimes prepared to make a gesture—such as granting an interview to a research worker or technical college teacher, or making a donation of a machine or money towards a technical college—but not much more.

Even where training departments existed and arrangements were regularly made to have staff trained externally, top managements had mixed feelings about them. Sometimes top management wanted to do the 'done' thing—to have a training department, to put in an appearance at gatherings where many firms were represented, and to reward people by giving them the cachet of attendance at a course. Such ambivalence was also evident in the priority of production over training; where there was conflict, immediate production took precedence. Training courses were sometimes used to take up slack time, to do something with an individual at an awkward stage of his career, or to get an outside assessment of his abilities or potentialities, rather than to increase the man's competence.

Each firm pointed to its own special production techniques and its own operational problems and evinced doubt about the contribution that could be made by external organizations lacking experience of their own type of concern.

RELATIONS WITH TECHNICAL COLLEGES

The Status of Technical Colleges

Considerable reservations were expressed about the contribution technical colleges could make toward the day-to-day affairs of industry. The firms were somewhat astonished that their local college was deliberately seeking to do something for them; in almost every case they had assumed that the approach made by ourselves as a research team, working in collaboration with the local technical colleges, meant that they would be asked to do something for the college. It was almost as if they were service organizations to the college, providing them with students, data, and advice or help, rather than the college being expected to be useful to them.

These reactions must be considered in the context of the relative status within the community of technical colleges and firms and of the individuals that each employs. Though educational and scientific pursuits rank fairly high as social activities in Britain, the status of technical colleges among them is low. Rightly or wrongly, they are thought to serve a less important purpose than more 'academic' institutions, and to be concerned more with training in specific craft skills than with the general preparation of young people for life or for positions of social leadership and responsibility. By and large their teaching staff are regarded as experts on subjects lacking university status or as experts in established subjects whose abilities have not earned them posts in universities.

The Picture of the Teacher

The ways in which executives thought about the colleges and their staff, and especially about those who taught management and production engineering subjects varied a great deal, but certain significant consistencies could be identified.

The technical college teacher was seen more as school teacher than university lecturer and as a person of mediocre calibre. He was viewed as a member of a small and not very powerful organization, closely bound by regulations. His time was not regarded as precious. He was thought to be insufficiently appreciative of production viewpoints, 'up in the air', and over-theoretical.

It was often said that a man who really knew management and could practise what he preached would be a manager, not a teacher. Attitudes were quite often unrelated to particular individuals at local colleges. Generalizations appeared to be based on a few past experiences of college teachers, on hearsay, or on vague beliefs. The picture of the teacher was determined partly by certain indirect considerations. Teaching and research into human behaviour as something which can be systematically studied or can be changed tend to arouse anxiety and defensiveness; this often takes the form of acute criticism of the teacher or social research worker. It seemed to be partly this which called forth the frequent comment that the average teacher of management knew less about his subject than a good full-time manager. This view serves to anticipate possible criticism of local standards of management and production control. In a sense, the very frequency of criticism of the teacher is a tribute to him. When its purpose is to anticipate criticism by him it is an indication of respect for his opinions. Our ideas about others are often determined more by our own position and our own needs than by external reality. Executives' ideas about technical college teachers sometimes included elements apparently designed to protect their own ideas about themselves. When they said, as they frequently did, that 'those who can, do, and those who cannot, teach' they may have been reassuring themselves at the same time as they were casting doubt on the practical aptitude of the teachers.

Not all the ideas about the management teachers were, of course, negative. Comments were made which indicated his prestige as an educated and experienced person with something to contribute to the world of affairs. It was notable, however, that the senior executive did not see the potential contribution of the technical college teacher of management and production engineering subjects as a substantial one, and saw it as relating chiefly to others especially to junior supervisory grades.

Attitudes towards Formal Training in Management

Closely bound up with attitudes towards the teacher of management studies or production engineering and his usefulness, was the question of the value of formal training or qualifications in management subjects. Several of the firms were sponsoring one or another form of training in management or supervision, yet expressed considerable doubt whether formal training in these spheres could be helpful. This attitude was sometimes expressed by the person responsible for training programmes, as an indication of his own reservations. In other cases it was left to others in the firm to express the unfavourable attitudes.

Doubts arose from the speaker's commonsense knowledge of personality limitations in individuals, his feeling that the teacher who really knew anything about management would in fact be filling a managerial role, and his knowledge that management courses supply relatively few precepts as practical and specific as those in technical textbooks. As one senior supervisor said, 'You cannot look up "Chap playing up, what to do about" in the same way as you might seek a solution to a practical problem in Machineries' Handbook.'

Scepticism also derives from the spontaneous resistance with which people react to the idea that their efficiency can be improved, or that improvements in the way people get on together can be achieved through deliberate intervention or re-training. These are challenging notions with critical undertones. Assistance with problems having to do with relations between people is inhibited by the implication that the person requiring the assistance does not understand enough about himself and others. This is often regarded as a reflection on him as a human being, rather than as a recognition of the fact that one person might be more expert than another in a technical field. As an example, several managers met by the research team preferred to select staff for posts entailing social responsibility through one personal interview rather than through more systematic procedures in common use today.

Statements that psychology and sociology, which underlie management studies, do not contain principles in the same way as the physical sciences express in part a fear that some such general principles do in fact exist. This is a rather frightening notion it suggests that one's own behaviour is deficient if one does not know them, and also that these principles could be used by others to control or manipulate oneself. Most people hate that idea.

Another factor apparently inhibiting practical industrialists from using or recognizing the possible value of outside help in managerial and supervisory training and in social and psychological aspects of production and administration, was a confusion of the behavioural sciences underlying management subjects with social welfare and pure kindness. This confusion has been accentuated and to some extent caused in this country and the U.S.A. by the application of the term 'human relations' to describe work carried out in industry by specialists with professional qualifications in psychology, sociology, and allied subjects. Managements tend to react to the idea of advice and teaching by such specialists as if this implies that they are insufficiently kind to their employees or as if unusual friction exists in their staff relations.

Relations with the Management Department of Acton Technical College

We have been dealing with the attitudes of managements to personnel and training matters in general and towards training in management, supervision, and production engineering in particular. The local college, Acton Technical College, was regarded as one among many organizations competing for a limited market of students.

Managers in some firms had a good deal of contact with one or another of the departments of the College, in particular with its large engineering departments. Few managers and supervisors had much knowledge about the precise activities of the College or about its departments and courses. Several thought the College was only or mainly a night school for students who had failed to attain school-leaving standards at the proper age, or a place for young apprentices, or they believed that staff taught children by day and adults in the evenings. Some were astonished to hear that management subjects and production engineering were taught. They did not know the names of the staff concerned, and were pleasantly surprised to hear of their qualifications, background, and experience.

It was clear that a pronounced gap existed between industrial firms and large segments of the local institution aiming to assist them with training.

This general background material collected from the firms around the College, was supplemented by more detailed studies undertaken within three firms. Two of them were large firms, called here Food Manufacturers Ltd and Household Appliances Ltd; the third a small firm is called Engineering Servicing Ltd. These studies established more precisely what the firms wanted in training for management, supervision, and production engineering, and how the Management Department of the College fitted—or did not fit—into this picture.

REQUIREMENTS OF TWO LARGE MANUFACTURING FIRMS

The two larger firms had considerable resources of their own. Food Manufacturers Ltd had access to the training, personnel, and production engineering departments of the larger concern of which it was part, as well as its own personnel department. It also had a small, newly established work study department. The other firm had large and well-established departments in all three fields. Broadly speaking, neither firm felt any acute need for continuous, systematic external training. Their demands for external aid were sporadic and on a small scale.

Special Training and Outside Stimulation

Occasionally some new development—such as the introduction of a work study department—made it advisable for the firm either to recruit a specialist, or to have an employee trained by some outside specialist organization, or perhaps both.

It was felt to be healthy for a firm to send senior or promising members to be trained outside, sometimes by consultants, for the sake of the experience itself. A better quality course would naturally be preferred to an indifferent one, but it was felt to be beneficial for a staff member to participate for a time in a new environment, and meet executives from other firms. Household Appliances Ltd tried, for instance, to send one senior staff member to each Henley Administrative Staff College course, and also supplemented their junior supervisory staff training programme with similar outside experience. Even though it was considered to be largely the course members themselves who taught each other in such external events—especially those for senior managers—it was clearly felt that this experience was in itself of considerable value.

Both types of course mentioned above—providing special training and providing social stimulation—were seen by management and staff to have a positive value. It was noteworthy that those who had been away to courses, though they were often critical of particular teachers or arrangements, were usually pleased that they had gone. They felt they had benefitted, though they were sometimes hard put to describe what they had learned.

Acceptability of Training for Juniors

Sponsored staff training was more acceptable for junior supervisory staff than for other grades of employees. Household Appliances Ltd had comprehensive arrangements for junior supervisory training, both inside and outside the firm. At Food Manufacturers Ltd, where training schemes were less developed, a major part of the interest in the research project was aroused by the possibility that it might lead to some form of training for supervisors.

The need for the improvement of social, organizational, and

technical skills was more easily accepted for junior than for middle grade staff. Juniors were less skilled, and were not in a position to deny their need, but at the same time, there was an element of 'projection', namely the attribution to them of needs which their superiors found it difficult to admit as existing in themselves.

So far as training for others was concerned, most emphasis seemed to be on a need for advanced training for senior men. This suggests that senior managers felt secure enough to recognize that their skills could be improved.

Voluntary Attendance at Classes

Many employees of each firm attended courses on their own initiative. Naturally, these were evening classes, and were either at the technical college near the firm or near the homes of those concerned. The firms always knew of some employees who were attending such classes and were sometimes helping them, e.g. by paying their fees or slightly rearranging their hours of work. They correctly surmised that there were other employees attending evening classes without their formal sponsorship or knowledge.

While managements often expressed the view that the hopes of promotion that some such employees entertained were vain, they approved firmly of the idea that outside training facilities should exist for those willing to study on their own initiative and in their own time, in the hope that they would increase their knowledge and effectiveness and advance their careers.

Training Versus Production

Where employees were released for training, employers wanted minimum dislocation of production. Largely for this reason, they liked the ideas of having lecturers coming to teach on their premises,[1] and were specially interested in the facilities of the local technical college. It became clear that there lay behind the majority of formal releases for training a story of considerable negotiation, often between a training department and the production section concerned, before the release was actually achieved.

We had no doubt that more employees would be released for

[1] There is, however, also an implication in this preference that employees' time is more valuable than teachers'.

training if the policies of personnel and training departments were more acceptable to other departments in the firm or to the higher managements that oversee them all.

Choosing the Trainers

Food Manufacturers Ltd being part of a much larger concern, had a threefold choice for training facilities. These could be their own internal facilities, the facilities of the larger concern, and the facilities of external organizations. The seniority and competence of an individual chosen for training helped to determine where he would go. If his own firm, or the concern, seemed to have little more to teach him he might be trained outside. Concern facilities were, however, thought to have the advantage of emphasizing regularities in practice throughout the concern. The advantages of an internal course, run by the firm—such as the lecturer's knowledge of its members and of the firm, and the opportunity for intra-staff communication, and for the building up of company solidarity—are weighed against the general broadening, the stimulus and specialized competence available through outside organizations.[2]

Both firms required some basic similarity in outlook between themselves and the training institutions to which they sent their employees. They looked with disfavour upon courses giving what they considered to be undue emphasis to one or other aspects of a subject in which they were interested. Both made careful assessments of the quality of the courses available.

When managements invest in training they try to do so as shrewdly and as economically as in anything else. They assess the relative costs of the alternative courses offered, the facilities of the training organization, and the qualifications, experience, calibre, and practical understanding of its teaching staff. In some respects, these decisions were taken with even greater caution than ordinary commercial transactions. This is because the firms were by no means unanimously, unambiguously 'sold' on the possibilities of training in supervision and management, or even in the more firmly established field of work study.

[2] To some extent, of course, external and internal courses are complementary or are appropriate for different subjects or levels of staff.

Work with the Acton Management Department

While there were gaps in the knowledge of the personnel and training departments of the two firms about the Acton Management Department, they knew more than most other firms, and had met some staff members. Neither firm was enthusiastic—on first contact—about the possibilities of increased work with the Department.

Within Food Manufacturers Ltd, the Department was thought unlikely to stand up to comparison with internal concern facilities or other external institutions. The Department was not considered able to make a contribution to the firm's special problems in view of the College's known emphasis on engineering and of the lack of knowledge of the firm's processes and management. Line managers especially felt that the qualities of responsibility, adaptability, and understanding important to a manager could not be developed by external training and that a good general education, together with a sound technical knowledge of manufacturing or sales processes, were really more useful. There had, moreover, been a limited recent contact with the Department that had led the firm to doubt whether the teachers were practical enough in their orientation and were pitching their courses at the right level. However, the personnel and work study divisions were prepared to persevere with the Department and learn more about it, and to spend time with teachers in the hope that something of value would eventuate.

In Household Appliances Ltd, there was a much larger personnel and training department. There was also a comprehensive internal training programme. Supervisory training was well established and based on considerable experience, and it was thought unlikely that any technical college department could compete with their own well-organized and long-established courses. Technical college salaries were regarded as too low to attract good managers as teachers.

While outside courses were used. it was not regarded as a serious proposition to send people above the rank of foreman to Acton for a managerial training. It was widely thought that personal qualities combined with technical knowledge and the right sort of practical experience on the job of the kind provided within the firm were the best preparation for a promising young manager.

The company preferred to run its own courses in 'tool' subjects, as these were so much influenced by company practice, and it was thought that its own very large and well known work study department could do far more for selected employees than the Acton Department.

Paradoxically, the technical college was considered to provide more important opportunities for training by teaching. Evening lecturing was thought to help a staff member to clarify his thoughts and increase his ability to present information and handle groups—facilities held in high regard in industrial fields. (There were several members of the firm teaching part-time at the College.)

While executives in the firm were pleased that students could attend classes at Acton on their own initiative, they required convincing that the Department could offer something they did not themselves supply if they were to make more use of its services.

THE REQUIREMENTS OF A SMALL ENGINEERING FIRM

Limitation of Resources

Much of what has been said above about the training needs felt by the larger firms was true of the small firm. There existed here the same ambivalence towards outside assistance; the same doubts about help in major matters of organization, and a similar emphasis on the training needs of junior supervisory staff.

Several factors, however, differentiated Engineering Servicing Ltd from the larger firms. They did not make an end-product of their own but components for other firms, and were entirely dependent upon services to other firms. They were, therefore, concerned to keep as much of their resources as possible at the daily disposal of customers. The firm was so small, and skill so unevenly distributed, that the absence of two or three people could dislocate a production schedule. Some commitments were completely dependent on the availability of particular men for whom substitutes were not available. While releases from production duties would have been easier if there had been an internal training department on the same premises, the firm was too small for such a department to be economical.

Need for Aid

At the same time, a much more acute need for external advice and help was evident than in either of the larger firms studied. This was largely because of the rate and manner in which the firm had grown. Growth had been dependent on immediate ability to meet fresh commitments; this had led to the promotion to supervisors and managers of those employees nearest at hand. As a result, key positions were occupied by relatively untrained employees whose technical and organizing competence (in their own opinion, as well as in that of management) left much room for improvement.

Moreover, the firm appeared to have reached a critical stage in its development at which it was just too large to function effectively on the informal and personal basis on which it had been built. Improvisation had to be replaced by organization. Investment in machines and premises increased capacity for production, but was, concurrently, aggravating the problem by increasing the need for more effective modes of organization and more efficient supervision and training.

Understanding Training Needs

Engineering Servicing Ltd were just beginning to feel their way towards external assistance. They had made inquiries into possible training for a newly promoted foreman and had made an approach to the Department of Management and Production Engineering. A teacher in the Department and one of us made more detailed inquiries. These showed that it was not only the foreman who needed training, and that any course needed to include both technical and organizational components. Many employees at foreman and chargehand level had gaps in their general and technical education and could profit from training in methods of work simplification, costing, and supervision. Their conceptions of the proper functions of a foreman were inadequate and they over-emphasized the part played by technical knowledge and by actual production work in successful supervision. The idea was widespread that production depended almost entirely on machinists. At a meeting held with supervisors one said that it was easier to spare a foreman than a machinist for training during work hours, as the presence of the foreman was less important for production. No-one contradicted him.

It was difficult to decide whom to train. Even the rumour that two employees were likely to receive training had started speculation about who these would be, and should be, and what this would mean to them and to others. Prospective trainees and others wondered if the plan implied a critical comment on their own ability, whether they would absorb all the training, and whether they would have the opportunity to apply what they had learned.

This illustrated one of the major features of the firm, that its structure was not best organized to provide the degree of flexibility that was demanded by its processes, by its relations with customers, and by its rate of growth. The decision to seek outside help in matters of training and organization was indeed a realistic one.

THE LIMITED DEMAND FOR TRAINING

To summarize, the larger firms, with their own considerable resources, felt little or no need for the services of such departments as the Acton Management Department beyond a service in the form of straightforward classes for junior supervisory staff in the application of methods engineering techniques and 'management' subjects of the conventional type. They preferred to hire, or send senior or potentially senior staff to study under, specialists of greater proven experience and skill. The smaller firm felt a need for staff training and, to some extent, for external consultant advice on matters of organization and production; but management was hesitant to invest a significant proportion of its resources in training, returns from which were felt to be uncertain, intangible, and, even if realizable, probably so only in the long term. The main needs of the staff of the firm were for courses or special tuition in the organization and supervision of production. Also, some wanted classes on such topics as elementary trigonometry, the use of logarithms, and slide-rule working to enable them to remedy deficiencies in general or technical education that they now regretted.

CHAPTER IV

The Teacher and his Tasks

At the beginning of the study the full-time staff of the Department consisted of a Head (responsible to the Principal for the organization and conduct of the work of the Department), with a senior lecturer, two lecturers, and an assistant. During the project, a second senior lecturer and a third lecturer were appointed. There were also twenty-five part-time lecturers and a full-time laboratory steward.

The qualifications and previous experience of the full-time staff are set out below.

QUALIFICATIONS OF DEPARTMENTAL TEACHING STAFF

Post	*Educational or professional qualifications*	*Experience prior to College teaching*
Departmental head	M.A. (English)	Post-graduate work in experimental psychology Commisioned Army service Administration in Germany with A.M.G.O.T.
Senior lecturer in production engineering[1]	A.M.I. Mech. E. A.M.I.P.E.	Experience in industry

[1] Author of a text-book on his subject.

Post	*Educational or professional qualifications*	*Experience prior to College teaching*
Lecturer in production engineering	A.M.I. Mech. E. A.M.I.P.E. AFR. AE. S.	Experience in industry Teaching in a university college
Assistant (later promoted lecturer)	B.Sc. (electrical engineering) (psychology) Grad. I.E.E.	Experience in industry Social research in industrial problems
Lecturer in management (left during project)	B.Sc. (Econ.) LL.B.	Social research in industrial problems Legal practice in U.S.A.
Lecturer in management (appointed during project, later promoted senior lecturer)	B.A. (history) Teacher's Training Certificate	Adult education in U.K. and U.S.A. Experience in industry
Lecturer in management[1] (appointed during project)	M.Sc., Ph.D. (sociology)	University lecturer
Assistant lecturer in management	B.Com.Sc. B.Ed.	Clinical psychologist Social research

Financial Rewards

New salary levels were approved for technical college teachers in 1956. The new salary scales gave £850 per annum to a man with the minimum qualifications the Department would be willing to accept and £1,750 to the Head of the Department. During the project before that date, salaries ranged from about £800 per annum for the assistant, to £1,300 per annum for the Departmental Head.[2] The range between the starting-points and the

[1] Author of a book on military organization.

[2] Approximate salaries only have been given here, as the exact salary of an individual is affected by a variety of special factors such as possession of a degree or professional qualification and number of years of previous experience.

top levels of the salary scales of technical college teachers has therefore risen, but is still comparatively narrow. A new teacher started with more than a university lecturer, but his ceiling was lower than that of the lecturer and of some school-teachers. Salaries are lower and prospects more limited than in industrial and commercial posts requiring comparable qualifications and experience, though the teacher has longer holidays and greater security of tenure. Although most people would consider the longer holidays an advantage, these are, of course, commonly considered to be necessary for teachers because of the complex and intensive nature of their relations with those they teach.

Hours of Work

Technical college teachers employed by Middlesex County Council are required to work thirty-nine weeks of thirty hours each per annum. Like all teachers in Middlesex colleges, a teacher in the Management Department is required by his employers to spend approximately two-thirds of his duty time in face-to-face teaching, and expected to spend most of the rest preparing lectures and organizing his work.

He may undertake research during that part of his duty time outside the required face-to-face teaching hours if he has time for it and may apply for remission of part of the teaching hours for this purpose. He is free to undertake research or consulting outside his duty hours during term time and during his thirteen weeks of formal vacation.[1] He may be released for several months to work in industry, if his colleagues will take over his work for him.[2]

Attitudes to the Work of the Department

Members of the Department were determined to reconsider the Department's current services, and were willing to change them radically if this appeared necessary. This outlook was expressed in the initiation of the research project to study De-

[1] The teacher may use College apparatus or material for these purposes and is entitled to half the fees, the other half going to the local authority.

[2] While there is no County provision for this, Acton Technical College has sometimes been able to arrange to appoint a temporary substitute in such cases.

partmental services and relationships, and in the appointments that were made to the staff of young people in contact with the most modern approaches in the social sciences. There was an eagerness to experiment in the hope that the services offered could reflect the progress beginning to be made in these matters elsewhere, in Britain and in the United States.

This did not mean that the reputation of Acton was poor. It had a high reputation. But industrialists and teachers have questioned for some years the value of conventional approaches to management and supervisory training and to the application of production engineering techniques. When the post of Head of Department was vacated in 1952 by an eminent production engineer well known for his critical approach to many traditional techniques, the College decided to continue the policy of critical evaluation and to intensify attempts to make the teaching of management and production engineering subjects more meaningful and practical. The College took the opportunity to appoint as Head a man who had held a senior rank during the war, and had an academic background and an interest in experimental and social psychology, giving him with his appointment an implied mandate to explore new and more effective kinds of work with students and firms.

At the time of the study, these attempts had been going on for less than a year. They continued during the two-year research project, changing their direction and pace as experience was gained, as research data pointed to new needs, and as the research team helped with changes.

While the following sections identify endemic features of the Department's relations rather than the developmental efforts by the Department, which are described later, they are coloured by its own special approach to management teaching and its desire to launch new enterprises.

RELATIONS WITH STUDENTS

Learning about Human Behaviour

Efforts to teach people about human behaviour face severe difficulty. The student finds that he is being required to deal in an unfamiliar way with apparently familiar events. Where he saw only people and life in taken-for-granted terms, he is being asked to look at these in a different way, to think in terms of such abstract concepts as roles, relations, structure, culture, situation, function, and process. He is encouraged to seek explanations for social events less in terms of physical facts and the personal idiosyncrasies of those around him, and more in terms of group collaboration towards solutions to technical and economic problems. He has to become aware that the particular group and personal difficulties that he experiences are rarely purely idiosyncratic or accidental, but in some degree explicable in terms of social and psychological causes.

If he becomes more sensitive to causes and consequences he should be better able to devise administrative actions, and to deal with business problems and better able to anticipate reactions to policies and practices.

It is particularly difficult to get students in a department of management and production engineering to re-orient their thinking in this way. They have a technical background. They work with concrete things. The regularities of human behaviour are abstract ideas. Moreover, much of what is known about individual and group behaviour is diffused. There are few precise theories of the kind that exist in engineering and physics and can be learned and then applied to examples with readily visible results. Often it is challenging and threatening to find that personal biases as much as reality are determining assessments of situations.

In the Department of Management and Production Engineering, in addition to these problems of teaching about behaviour, there were difficulties related to the kinds of student attracted. While intellectual standards were high, several students lacked the personal qualifications for promotion to management. They pinned too much hope on courses and qualifications in management studies. Teachers in the Department described how some students would sit in a class and wait to be lectured at. In doing so they were, of course, exhibiting the very characteristic—undue dependence—that inhibited further progress towards the assumption of managerial responsibilities.

The Teacher's Dilemma

Our individual interviews with students confirmed that many were vague about what academic courses could, and could not, do for them. They were more dependent and less certain than one would expect potential managers to be. They had inaccurate conceptions of themselves to match against the positions they wanted to take up in industry. It could be held that the Department was responsible only for formal instruction and for helping students to understand the intellectual content of classroom instruction and literature. The formal obligation of technical colleges is to admit those applicants with the capacity to profit from attendance at the classes given. It is not part of this obligation to cooperate in any more active manner in furthering the student's career and in developing personal attributes that would help him. And yet—and this was the major dilemma of the Department's teaching in management studies—the ability to work well with others and to lead working groups depends only partly on specific technical skills acquirable through academic study and experience. Personal qualities are of paramount importance.

People of a given age do not all have the same potential for management, but it is probably true that almost anyone who is intelligent, educated, and within the normal variation of personality, can be helped to develop such capacities as he has for taking additional responsibilities. The problem of the Department was to decide how far to stick to a narrow interpretation of the regulations, lecturing to the students and leaving it at that, and how far to venture into the realm of personal help to students.

Few management skills are of the type that can be given by one person to another; they often require the student to abandon dependent or defensive modes of behaviour, and they, like everyone else, are very reluctant to give these up. This is one of the central problems in management teaching. Teachers have continually to decide how far to go with the student as an individual, and to devise approaches which, while being genuinely helpful to the student, are within the teacher's own competence, and legitimate within a college context.

The distinction between education for management and attempted psychological therapy was difficult to draw. Yet the teacher dared not err, for fear of turning an educational establishment into a disguised psychiatric clinic, or of raising psychiatric problems for the resolution of which he could not accept responsibility.

The circumstances in which teachers and students were brought together were not always propitious for their joint task. Members of the Management Department had to sustain complex and demanding relations with large numbers of students. Some had to be kept up over a period of years, but short courses, e.g. in methods engineering, brought several separate groups into the Department for brief periods every year. The teacher had quickly to form close and productive relations with each group, then go on very soon to a fresh group also wanting something tangible from him over a period of weeks.

Methods engineering students were required to bring practical projects from their own works, on which they could work with fellow students and teachers. They presented as problems of physical process or layout what often turned out to be problems of social relations within the firms concerned. How far could the teacher go with the student in his analysis? Often he had to ask himself whether it was fair to show a student in a junior position how complicated the problem really was without being able to help him reconcile himself to the limited contribution that he could make to its solution from his position in the firm.

RELATIONS WITH FIRMS

Members of the Department met firms mainly through inquiries about arrangements for courses. Frequently a personnel or training officer telephoned or visited the Department to discuss the needs of employees and to learn what the Department might be able to offer.

At first glance such discussions might seem simple enough. Often, however, they became complex. First, it was often difficult for the industrial representative to explain, or the teacher to understand, exactly what the prospective students needed. The firm's representative was not always able to put this into words; proper understanding by the teacher often seemed to require first-hand experience both of the works and of the people concerned. Second, the training officer often differed from colleagues in his own firm about what was required, and this difference might not have been adequately resolved in the firm before the visit to the College. Third, the ideas of the training officer and the teacher might differ. A firm might, for example, ask the Department to 'train foremen to handle shop stewards.'

For the teacher to accept this request at face value would be unconstructive. It would assume that a shop steward is a special kind of human being different from others and susceptible to certain prescribed techniques of manipulation. It would be more comfortable for the teacher not to point this out, but this would evade the issue for the sake of appearing helpful.

New ideas about the employees' needs might emerge from the discussion, and it might take several meetings before sufficient agreement could be reached to make some workable arrangement.

These discussions and negotiations were often delicate. In describing the situation of the firm and the training needs of students, the training officer would often present what appeared to the teacher to be implicit consulting problems relating to the firm as a whole, or to the training officer's responsibilities, rather than relatively narrow teaching problems relating to small groups of students. This was a challenge for the teacher; while it was easier and safer to deal with the narrower, more specific teaching problem with which help was formally requested, the situation sometimes seemed to cry out for more fundamental forms of help of a type he was very anxious to give, e.g. concerning matters of general management and organization and reactions to administrative changes. On the other hand, it was not formally for this that the training officer had come to him and he might be affronted by an explicit offer. If any such arrangements were made the initiative had to come from the firm and the teacher had to be quite sure in his own mind that he would be tackling something comfortably within his technical competence and within his terms of reference as a staff member of a technical college.

On some occasions a teaching component would enter into the discussions themselves; the training officer's understanding of the problems of his firm and of students might be clarified as he attempted to explain them to the teacher or as the teacher commented upon them.

On other occasions the training officer would go away, convinced that he or his firm had more to offer the student than the teacher could provide. The unimpressive physical environment of the Department,[1] the novel views of several staff members and the determination to clarify their roles and the work they could usefully do sometimes strengthened this impression. Matters were not made easier by the known ambivalence of industrial executive towards teachers of management subjects. At the same time it must be borne in mind that the teacher tended to be over-anxious to show what he could do and to prove that, despite his lesser practical experience, he could be of value to the students and their employers.

When it seemed that the Department could provide a useful service for students sponsored by the firms, the teacher had to fit the students into an existing or prospective course, or to design a new course and secure time to prepare and give it. He had to make sufficient staff time available. It was often clear at this stage that the firms would become impatient with the relative inflexibility of public institutions and the inevitable delays in meeting unusual or rapidly expanded demands.

COMMON ELEMENTS IN RELATIONS WITH STUDENTS AND EMPLOYERS

Attitudes to the Outside 'Expert'

The relations that the teacher made with students and with representatives of firms had important characteristics in common. However anxious a student or organization may be to use the services of a teacher or adviser, there is always some mixture of feelings towards calling him in to help with a problem, even though this is not always put into words. The positive feelings make the teacher's or adviser's work possible, provided that undue dependence is avoided. Use of his services constitutes recognition that he may be able to help increase the knowledge of

[1] There is no doubt that the physical environment of the Department detracted from the dignity of those who work in it, in the eyes of visitors and students. On the other hand, it is interesting to note the finding of the Department and research team that the older employees met in the small firm that provided one of the industrial case studies were made rather nervous at the possibility of having to display their ignorance in "grand" buildings. It is no doubt possible to have the best of both worlds by having reasonable buildings and at the same time working initially with some groups of employees outside the College.

those who call upon him or help them towards more appropriate and effective behaviour. On the other hand his work arouses anxieties, because it brings people up against the gaps in their knowledge and suggests that they may have to abandon familiar ways of behaviour in favour of new ways, of whose advantages they cannot be certain.

Furthermore, the outside person often has to clarify the situation with which he is trying to help. In work with organizations he usually has to open informal as well as formal channels of communication. This often has the result of revealing doubts and unresolved difficulties that the persons concerned have preferred to deny, retain as their private property, or make unspoken agreements not to display. For this reason it seems that he is creating trouble.

For such a complex of reasons some degree of hostility tends to be focussed on him as one who brings unpopular information to light, makes explicit what it is preferred to leave implicit, and adds to the responsibilities of those in the organization. Directing hostility on to the teacher serves at the same time to help the individual avoid his own doubts or to help the organization avoid facing its own internal divisions and difficulties and to protect its internal solidarity.

Tolerating Ambivalence

The strength and mode of expression of the negative feelings vary between individuals and through time, sometimes taking the form of a mild and friendly scepticism and sometimes an active (though perhaps unconscious) hostility to those whose knowledge or help is secured. These reactions seem to occur irrespective of the quality of the outside help, and irrespective of the degree of success secured through it.

Some measures of resentment are so common that the teacher or adviser has to be prepared to accommodate himself, as a matter of course, to a highly critical eye on him while he works. Indeed, capacity to tolerate long periods of spoken or unspoken criticism without becoming hurt, upset or angry, or diverted from one's purpose, is a *sine qua non* for successful teaching and advisory work. Most people are familiar with the mixture of feelings towards them on the part of someone who is learning from them (even if they have only had the experience of teaching someone to drive a car). This phenomenon will, therefore, be easily understood to exist among students.

The statement that organizations tend to regard outsiders with mixed feelings may seem a little strange. There are many key people in organizations who are extremely enthusiastic about training or external advisers and this enthusiasm seems unambiguous. The apparent lack of ambiguity on their part often seems balanced by a lack of enthusiasm or a scepticism felt by some other members of their own firms, who, in a manner of speaking, express the doubts of the enthusiast for himself.

RELATIONS WITH COLLEAGUES

Contacts with Part-time Staff

There were about three times as many part-time as full-time teachers. They were mainly industrial staff who spent up to six hours a week, usually in the evenings, teaching students. The ranks of the part-time teachers were seldom stable. The rewards were poor (up to three guineas for an evening's work). Although there existed some enthusiasts who were willing to teach for such nominal rewards, the full-time staff was faced with a chronic problem of securing and retaining suitable part-time teachers. Sometimes they simply could not do so and had to be content with lower standards than they liked, or with part-time teachers with whose approach they did not agree. Although this was formally the problem of the Departmental Head, it was widely shared by his colleagues. They often handled the same courses and students as the part-time teachers and were anxious to keep up appropriate standards. If a part-time teacher was thought by students to be below standard or uninterested in the work, it was, moreover, often the full-time staff as a whole that the firms and students blamed.

Apart from the problem of securing sufficient part-time teachers of satisfactory academic qualifications and teaching experience, the full-time staff were concerned that their contact with part-time staff was so limited. Full-time teachers worked mainly in the day-time and part-time teachers in the evening. It was often difficult for a part-time teacher to obtain time off from work to discuss a course during the day; the full-time staff had to wait some hours after their day's work was finished. Meetings between full- and part-time staff in pairs or as groups were additionally difficult to arrange because there was no way of paying for the time spent on such meetings—the only payments permitted to part-time staff were for part-time teaching and the same applied to full-time staff for work outside their official hours. Efforts were made at the sacrifice of time and money by both, but it was clear that there was insufficient contact between them and that this was militating against the development of common viewpoints and approaches.

Links with Colleagues in other Departments

Contact with colleges outside the Department was also uneven. It was, in general, only the teachers who had had some years in the Department who associated much with the rest of the College. This was partly because several members of the Department were new and had academic and practical backgrounds of a different kind from those of their colleagues. Insecurity of status of their subjects, their novelty in comparison with those dealt with by other departments, and the tendency they have to excite anxiety or a defensive amusement contributed to relative isolation. Also important appeared to be the determination of the Department, and especially the Departmental Head, to break away from the conventional in College work to something new in approach. This challenged traditional elements in the College outlook.

RELATIONS WITH COLLEGE AND COUNTY SUPERIORS

Difference between Formal Requirements and Actual Work

Our study of the activities of the teachers in the Department of Management and Production Engineering showed as its central feature a distinct difference between what the teacher was formally required by his employers to do and what he did.

First, the teacher spent less than the required proportion of hours in the formal face-to-face teaching of classes, but much more than that time in other work. This other work could also be broadly described as educational and was perhaps more so, for example advising students and their employers on training needs and possibilities, and helping and guiding the practical application of what was taught.

Second, time, inadequately allowed for officially, was being spent in visiting firms for these purposes and for acquiring greater familiarity with the workday environment of students.[1]

Third, much more seemed to be done in the way of course organization, advice to students and firms, and the development of professional competence and contact with colleagues—in the raising of standards—than appeared to be envisaged in the regulations.

This difference between practical reality and formal requirement was tolerated by the College and County Council authorities, though the staff would have liked much more active encouragement. In their voluntary effort to develop their services, the teachers had to tolerate uncertainty about the degree of sanction which much of their work received. Sometimes they felt frustrated about the differences in perception of needs and obligations between themselves and their superiors. They knew that in the last resort the authorities could have brought much of the experimental work of the Department to an end merely by invoking the regulations. Strains arose partly because of the existence of unresolved ambiguities and obscurities of definition in regulations governing teaching duties, visits to firms, research and consulting, and the amount of leeway informally allowed for these. They also arose because of the difficulties facing the staff in establishing new and only partly understood types of service for which there existed few precedents and little overt public demand and which offered few opportunities for the demonstration of spectacular short-term success.

DEMANDS AND SATISFACTIONS OF THE JOB

Much of the foregoing can be summarized in a resumé of the psychological demands of the job upon the teacher and the satisfaction which he derived from it.[2] He had to guide students through various possibilities of study open to them, some leading to paper qualifications of professional institutions, others devised on the spot in an attempt to maximize their practical benefit. It was essential that the teacher should be able to sustain

[1] If this type of work is to bear its best fruit and to be preserved for communication to others, it also requires detailed subsequent recording, which consumes at least as much time as the initial observations.

[2] The time referred to is primarily the first year of the research project.

a role towards which there was a great deal of mixed feeling. In his relations with students he had to be able to balance the inevitable unreality of certain of the students' demands against his ability to give them something of lasting benefit. He had to tolerate the strain of a situation where too much was demanded of him and too quickly. He had to be able to make an effective compromise between what the students thought they had come to acquire and what he thought they needed.

Subject though he was to multiple sources of suggestion and influence upon what he should teach (emanating from College committees and several professional institutions as well as 'consumers'), he had to make up his own mind about what would be useful to students and firms. He had to be able to tolerate the ambiguity of his position in the eyes of executives and to some extent in the eyes of his colleagues and superiors, since both groups tended to look with some doubt and uncertainty upon such new subjects as his, apparently vague in form and content and difficult to distinguish from common-sense, taken-for-granted behaviour precepts. He did not have high prestige in either the industrial or the educational world.

He had to be able to balance his responsibilities between individuals and groups and between students and employers and to maintain a large number of social relations, of which the majority were intensive and of short duration and not immediately practically productive. He had to reconcile himself to limitations in the extent to which students, executives, and his own superiors were prepared to collaborate with him.

On the other hand, the satisfactions and rewards of such a post successfully performed could be considerable. The teacher was not without prestige. While students were quick to criticize their teachers, they usually looked on them at the same time as experts who should not be doubted, as persons with considerable skill, experience, and knowledge, and as persons of great potential importance in helping them in their careers. Teachers received some satisfactions from developing individuals, helping them expand the limits of their universe, and from carrying a highly responsible, exacting, and many-sided role making great demands on the personality. Perhaps most important, the teacher had the stimulus of knowing that he was a member of a group trying to pioneer a new and enterprising type of service to students and industrial firms which, if successful, would be unique in the educational world.

CHAPTER V

The Development of Services to Students

The Department and the research team together studied the practical implications of emerging material and explored ways of improving services to students and firms. This new knowledge was added to experience of the staff. Certain priorities became clear. This chapter and the two that follow describe some of the main developmental attempts made by the Department, usually with the help of the research team, and records some successes and failures.

Increased efforts were needed to clarify with students, on joining the Department and during their studies, the relation between what the Department had and what students wanted. This would help them to choose on a more realistic basis exactly what courses to pursue, and to decide whether the Department had anything for them. Students needed help in working over and integrating into their outlook what they learned of different subjects and in relating what they learned in the classroom to their work. Teaching methods—or alternative forms of beneficial experience—were needed to help students learn and practise new forms of behaviour.

LEARNING BY ACTIVE PARTICIPATION

It would be difficult for any conscientious teacher, in the circumstances described in the previous chapter, to reconcile himself to a one-way system of teaching. This would perpetuate the limitation of the students and give the teacher a reputation as one whose efforts had little perceptible result. Inevitably, therefore, the teachers in the Department sought methods that, although beyond the minimum of their formal obligations, might really help students and satisfy their own consciences as teachers. They had to harness their knowledge and insight about group and individual behaviour to establish productive relations with their own students.

Group Discussion as a Teaching Method

The staff used guided group discussions extensively to supplement other methods of instruction on 'college' courses. This setting allows students more spontaneity than do formal lectures. They have a better chance to seek information as and when they want it and to absorb it at their own speed and in terms meaningful to them. In particular, learning about human behaviour often seems to occur more effectively in such a situation. The student can learn at two levels from the overt content of what is actually said and from the feelings and processes actually experienced within the group. He can observe, at first hand, resistances to new ideas that can teach him much about probable reactions when changes are suggested in industry.

An increased understanding of human interaction in group situations could be helpful to any student of management subjects. It was the deliberate intention of the Department to lead some groups of students along this road, helping them to understand group processes by clarifying these at both the overt and covert levels and by clarifying the roles assumed by the individual student in the group.

They found that this approach had to be used with great care. Students could easily be frightened away by the unconventionality of method. While students sometimes seemed to be gaining insight into group processes and their own behaviour in dealing with others, they were at other times puzzled about the methods used or hostile towards them and the teachers who used them. On occasion there seemed a possibility of increased dependence upon teachers for too long.

It became apparent that it would be all too easy to change the College from an educational to a quasi-psychiatric institution. This did not necessarily mean that the interpretations of group behaviour made by the teachers were wrong or that the method was being unsuccessful—such reactions to interpretative attempts to clarify behaviour are not unusual, whether or not the interpretations are apt, because they are in some way a comment on one's 'private' personality. But it raised problems, since contact with students on the 'college' courses was usually short-lived; over-sensitive responses could not always be guarded against and the implications of new insights absorbed. While the explicit exploration of students' reactions to each other and to their teachers might be most effective in improving their capacity to manage, the limitations of the teacher's role made this a difficult and possibly dangerous endeavour.

Through practice, consultation with other teachers of emotionally charged material, discussion with us, and experience of a course given at the Tavistock Institute, the staff seemed to improve their techniques and develop their abilities to use and convey insights during group discussion without necessarily making direct interpretations to individual students of the possible meanings of their own behaviour.

The techniques gave more opportunity to students to draw their own conclusions in their own time, under their own conditions, and on their own responsibility, following the general principle that the most potent, lasting, and helpful insights are those which group participants achieve on their own under permissive and encouraging guidance.

Project Methods

The Department also sought to make its teaching less academic and more practical by using project methods where possible. This was done particularly on methods study courses, where students were generally required to bring a practical problem from their firms to the College. After some introductory instruction, the individual student was required, with the help of fellow students and the collaboration and supervision of the course teachers, to seek a solution to the problem he had brought. Discussion of these projects often provided the best opportunity to clarify the social elements of the problem presented. Students could be shown that while the social context of a particular task was always affected by its technical requirements, the reverse was also true. Sometimes, as we have seen, it appeared that the problems had little to do with techniques of engineering and much with human interaction.

On some occasions teachers worked with students' projects on the premises of their employers in the real contexts where they arose. While sometimes productive, this method could sometimes pose more difficulties than it solved. This was partly because of the ambiguous status of the teacher; it became obscure whether he was in a teaching role to the student or a consultant role to the firm. Also, the very fact that social situations contribute towards methods engineering problems made it easy for the teacher to become involved in unsanctioned negotiations with a student's colleagues and employers.

As teachers became more experienced in working with firms, their judgement improved in distinguishing situations for helping students learn from those where they would quickly find themselves dealing with matters in which, as teachers, they had no right to intervene. A large part of the task consisted of illustrating to the student what was and was not possible for a teacher to do as a teacher. Inevitably, students often put pressure upon teachers to come into their firms to try and solve technical and social problems with which they had not been successful on their own and with which they thought a stranger with some skill and prestige might help.

THE NATURE OF COURSES

Curtailments and Developments

Changes in teaching methods were accompanied by changes in the scope and nature of the courses offered. The Department decided to curtail its work with some of the conventional management certificate courses, and to develop new courses in their place. In 1955-6, the first-year course leading to the British Institute of Management Intermediate Certificate was not given; and in 1956-7, the second-year course was discontinued. Applicants were offered alternative courses according to their qualifications and needs, as far as the Department could judge them. One of these alternative courses was the successor to the discontinued I.I.A. Foremanship and Works Supervision course. The new course, designed by the Department itself, was called 'Organization and Supervision of Production'. It was wider in scope, yet more closely related to the kind of training needs revealed during the industrial field studies described in Chapter III. This course was held in both day-time and evening versions. Alternatively, students with degrees or similar qualifications were allowed to enter the B.I.M. Diploma courses in the evenings, or to prepare for this by taking a special selection of intermediate subjects.

The Graduate Trainees' course of 1954-5 developed into a more comprehensive course in Production Management, which was designed in collaboration with local firms. Senior industrial staff, such as a technical director and a general works manager, were brought in temporarily as lecturers at particular points in the course. The Methods Engineering courses were divided into full-time one-month 'appreciation' courses for managers and senior specialists, and 'training' courses for work study practitioners, which spread the equivalent of six weeks' study over two full-time periods separated by a part-time spell of practical work. In 1956-7, they were re-named work study courses. The Entering Industry course was not repeated. A new course was introduced in practical training methods, for foremen. In 1956-7, courses in inspection were begun for Chief Inspectors and for engineering inspectors.

A four-year course in production technology was designed, but, up to the time of writing, not held. It is to be given in the new Brunel College of Technology and will be a 'sandwich' course, on which students spend six months in the College, and six months working in local firms. It will lead to the new Diploma in Technology.

Guiding the Selection of Courses

At the same time as changing its courses, the Department, in the interests of students, sought to exercise greater discretion in their acceptance of applicants for various classes and activities. A few applicants were not accepted into the classes they wished to enter, even where they had the required educational background. This was done on the grounds that they seemed unlikely to be helped by the course towards more effective behaviour.

The Department also sought to guide students more carefully into courses (at Acton and elsewhere) from which they would profit in a practical as well as an academic sense and encouraged them to make their own careful selections among the events available to them.

This took courage, as the prestige of a technical college

department depends partly on the quality of its work, but also to some extent on the numbers of students it can enrol, and the staff were willing to encourage students to go elsewhere.

The Need for Personal Help

The experiences of teachers with students posed the problem of dealing with those who were not only, or not at all, seeking academic instruction, but needed some form of more personal help for at least part of their time. Many young people show a need for support and, wittingly or unwittingly, use academic as well as other contacts to try to obtain it. In adolescence and early adulthood they go through critical stages, passing from childhood, with its more-or-less protected family situations, to adult life with all this entails in economic independence and the formation of mature personal relations. National Service and, increasingly, university life help to provide young men with transitional communities between the home and the wider world. Some have lesser opportunities or do not manage to complete early maturation processes at the stage at which our society expects them to do so. It is not surprising, therefore, that a Department dealing mainly with young men at early stages of their careers is faced with such problems. This is accentuated by the fact that management training itself must set out to give some assistance in personal development. A further complication was that some students came to the Department to settle doubts about themselves.

Responsible teachers in a management department could not ignore these problems. Their own teaching methods even served sometimes dramatically to highlight them. After thorough consideration by the Department and ourselves, a consensus of opinion emerged that quasi-therapeutic complications should, as far as possible, be avoided in teaching, but that a beginning should be made with an alternative way of meeting these needs. It was not intended to set up a psychiatric service for students with personality difficulties. Students should be helped to judge clearly what the Department could or could not do for them and, if they wished, be told about other academic institutions and vocational guidance and clinical institutions outside the College that they might decide to use. This work with students was clearly extremely delicate and probably best in the hands of someone with appropriate clinical experience. Such a person is experienced in letting people express themselves to him and in understanding the communications they are making, and also in judging between permissible advice and comment on the one hand and psychotherapy on the other.

Counselling as a Personal Service

Fortunately the Department was able to start this work with the part-time services of a Departmental teacher who had past training and experience in clinical psychology. The new service to students, instituted in 1955, was called Student Counselling. The purpose of the service was to provide opportunities for current and prospective students in the Department to discuss the bearing that the facilities in the Department (or the College) might or might not have on their careers. The teacher seconded to this work tried to give the minimum of direct advice to the student. He tried rather to help the student clear his own mind about what he wanted from the Department and to make a realistic assessment about whether or not he was likely to get it. It was felt that if the student was helped to clarify his own problems and helped to find his own solutions to them he would benefit more than if ready-made solutions were offered to him.

The duties of the student counsellor came to include not only guidance and help to individual students, but also a range of coordinating duties that complemented the work of the new course tutors, described below. The counsellor was available at regular times, and by appointment, and was approached by students requiring widely varied forms of help. Particularly at at the beginning of sessions, he helped prospective students to see how courses in the Department might meet their requirements. Usually he discussed the student's present job, and any promotion or change of job he might be seeking, to try to formulate the sorts of skill, knowledge, and qualifications he might require.

Sometimes the counsellor has introduced students to other colleges when more suitable facilities seemed to be available there, and sometimes he has suggested to students who have just changed their jobs that they might best devote their energies, for the time being, to learning and tackling the new job, rather than to a course. Such an outcome to a discussion does not raise the student population of the Department, but probably gives the student more help than any course. The counsellor has also interviewed students who have not been accepted for courses, to discuss the reasons for this, and the alternatives open to them.

Students in the Department have approached the Counsellor, or have been referred to him by their tutors, when they have wanted to change their course, or have failed an examination and wish to discuss next steps, or when they are resuming studies after a long break. Students transferring from other colleges are helped to catch up and settle in. These are primarily educational problems. An important part of the Counsellor's work has been to help students sort out educational from career and personal problems. He has, in a few appropriate cases, done this successfully enough for students with primarily personal problems to ask to be referred to a psychiatric clinic. He has built up contacts with some local firms which are in search of promising ex-students of the Department, and with a local Labour Exchange, where he has been able to discuss a student's capacities and experience and so help the officers to place him. Local firms have been helped to select suitable students for courses in the Department. In these ways, this service has begun to benefit students and to be a useful and productive extension of the personnel functions of the firms that employ them.

DEPARTMENTAL ORGANIZATION AS A TEACHING INSTRUMENT

It had also become increasingly clear from study of the relations between teachers and students that in the learning of management studies the actions of teachers speak louder than words. It was necessary to use the organization of courses and of the Department as implicit demonstrations of what good management could achieve. This helped students to feel secure and to reassure them that their teachers could practise what they preached and were, therefore, likely to improve their own practices. The Department could present a concrete lesson of how to cope with the administrative problems of a rather complicated institution with an unstable population.

This was vividly illustrated in a reorganization of enrolment. This transformed methods involving considerable waiting and inconvenience among potential students into an orderly and methodically phased system that seemed to contribute towards confidence in the teaching institution.

A major step was taken at the beginning of the 1955-6 academic session by the introduction of a Departmental tutorial system. This was operated by full-time staff members. Each tutor guided the work of teachers (especially part-time teachers) on a group of courses and sought to help sub-groups of the students on a course relate the different subjects within it to each other and to what they experienced in their firms. This system helped to clarify student needs and to improve communication between students and teachers. It provided students with a second channel of communication with Departmental staff and with someone specifically to consult about academic matters and about relations between the subjects they studied and their own practical experience. It also provided the teachers with an opportunity to show that, as specialists, they knew how to anticipate students' insecurity about learning and their anxiety about whether they would be able to apply what they learned.

The tutorial system met a major need in giving the Departmental Head administrative assistance, spreading supervisory responsibilities of the Department, and bringing the larger population of part-time teachers into more frequent contact with full-time staff members and their approaches and practices. As a teaching method, the tutorial system seemed to help the student by offering him a relation with one senior person different from that usually available between lecturers and students in large classes. The relation was potentially closer, and at the same time could cover a wider range of the student's purpose than the need to learn a particular subject.

CHAPTER VI

The Development of Services to Firms

We saw that industrial firms expected little from the Department and, in some ways, from their local technical college generally. Neither the Department nor the College were thought to exist for the sake of industry.[1] As we have said, many executives expected to be asked to do something for the College or Department; they were rather astonished that the object was to provide them with improved services. They saw themselves as suppliers of students, governors, part-time teachers, and donations to the College rather than as consumers and beneficiaries of college services.

Closer liaison was necessary with local firms, so that teachers could learn about the needs of firms and the environment of students and so that perceptions and training needs could be better shared between teacher and executive. Occasional formal meetings were not enough. Teachers and executives had to work together on joint tasks in which both had a stake. Real working partnerships between teacher and executive had to be constructed, in the course of which a respect for each other could develop and some interchange of knowledge and skill take place.

The Department needed to become a more open institution; teachers needed to develop personal links with firms, and execu-

[1] The definition in the Education Act, 1944, of the responsibilities of local education authorities suggests that the major responsibility of technical colleges is for adult education, but the policy of the Ministry of Education is that technical colleges should not only help students but also provide technical education that is required for industry. The Department and College and the County Council certainly wanted to help industry and made many arrangements about students with their employers.

tives to take a greater share of responsibility for what was taught in the College. Where the opportunities arose for research or consulting it was highly desirable that these should be taken, while the general service to firms and students could be maintained in the ordinary way through formal classes.

It seemed that the Department was more likely to develop new services by concentrating on the construction of links with a relatively small number of firms than by forming less intensive relations with a large number. Although the official College catchment area covered most of Middlesex and included a population of nearly two million, more than half of the Department's students were drawn from ten firms in and around the Acton borough. A nucleus of firms contributed large sections of the student body, had staff members who were governors or part-time teachers at the College, and had some contact with teachers in more than one department. Opportunities to build new services were most likely to develop where there was already some connection with a firm or where the Department could offer an improved way of meeting a need that was already known.

EARNING THE RIGHT TO WORK WITH FIRMS

Firms were extremely cautious in seeking or accepting help except in a limited range of topics. Where they did seek help they had mixed feelings about it. Nevertheless, an informal canvassing of possibilities by representatives of firms always went on; the firms contacted by the Department made innumerable conscious and unconscious explorations of what they might get from members of the Department. There was, however, a distinctly 'hard to get' atmosphere about such discussions; as we have stressed, the perceived possibilities of help with social or individual preoccupations is always simultaneously disquieting because it involves the prospect of giving up defensive mechanisms for unfamiliar alternatives.

The situation was naturally difficult for the Department to tolerate. Its members felt that often they could do more than they were being asked to do. It was frustrating to be confronted with tempting possibilities for challenging and interesting work and yet to be asked to do only relatively minor tasks of peripheral importance to the firm.

This position was exacerbated by the staff's belief that even narrowly defined training of junior employees requires an active partnership between College teachers and firms. The traditional farming out of students to colleges like incomplete components of a machine shop could never be adequate. At the same time only a limited range of activities in teaching, research, and consulting that might have been devised were appropriate for technical college departments and practicable within its organization and the framework of its rules.

Local firms were interested in new developments in the Department, when they became aware of these through junior employees who were students there, or through contacts with members of the Department and ourselves. They were puzzled as well as curious about the active wish of the Department to step outside its accustomed role, to learn their needs and work more closely with them, and a little sceptical about the benefits that might accrue from this. This sceptism derived not only from the attitudes to help from teachers and research workers in the field of human behaviour already discussed, but also from the doubts of industry about the calibre of those to be found in technical college management and production engineering departments.

There was some reality in this: highly experienced research workers and consultants in the field with which the Department was concerned are unlikely to be obtained 'ready made' at technical college salaries, and indeed are not usually sought for such posts. The firms were also sceptical about whether a technical college controlled by a local authority could give its staff the freedom and flexibility to engage in active work with industry outside the teaching of its junior employees.

In the earlier stages of the project the new contacts that firms had with the Department were often further complicated by difficulty in appreciating what the Department actually wanted to do. Departmental plans overestimated the amount and kind of work acceptable to firms and possible for staff in view of their qualifications and the nature of the administrative structure in which they were employed. Learning had to occur before more realistic assessments could be made of what was possible and how it was best to go about it. We helped by passing on selected material from industrial firms and by repeated discussions with the Department of practical implications for current and projected work with industry. There was inevitably considerable sensitivity about many of the points raised; we had to try to understand staff responses and to cope with resistances to information or suggestions where these necessitated uncomfortable changes in Departmental behaviour. The general tenor of these suggestions was that the Department was trying to do too much much too quickly. Some firms were discouraged from continuing with the Department even in conventional work. Sometimes the Department was forming plans to undertake more ambitious projects than the sttaff could be expected to cope with.

It became clear that the Department had to lower its sights, to safeguard its core of conventional, acceptable work, and to make pilot attempts within a few local firms, preferably on a small scale.

In so far as the Department wished to work with firms as whole units, the task confronting teachers was to build relations with firms in such a way that they earned the right to continued or expanding work. They had to show that they could tolerate circumscription of their efforts and wait for greater opportunities. They had to explore exactly how much scope they already had, or could secure, from their own employers, the County Council. All this was best done on well-defined and limited tasks. The most suitable tasks, it was decided, would be explicitly defined 'training surveys' in which the Department would study training needs with firms and report to them how far they could provide any necessary training or advice on training that was needed.

A TRAINING SURVEY

As reported earlier, one survey was designed and undertaken jointly by the Department and ourselves as a model for further similar efforts by the Department on its own. If an investment was to be made in training, the management of the firm 'Engineering Servicing Ltd', had to be quite certain that the precise needs of the man and the firm were understood by the teaching group and that he would learn sufficient to be able to make an increased contribution towards the organization as a whole. Discussions took place between the Departmental Head, the Managing Director of the firm, and a foreman, about the firm's and the individual's needs, and Departmental facilities. No current course or parts of courses seemed fully appropriate.

Outcome of the Investigation

Eventually, the Department and the firm decided to undertake with us a brief training survey designed to clarify training needs within the firm and the possible contribution that might be made by the Department. A report on the training survey was presented to a representative group of members of the firm and this was discussed in some detail. The group worked, with our help, towards a realization that external training could constitute as real an investment as purchase of a machine and that their doubts about such an investment related partly to uncertainty whether suggestions for change could peacefully be absorbed within the firm.

On the basis of observations within the firm, the Department was able to design a course in the organization and supervision of production especially tailored to the needs of the men and the firm concerned and those in similar circumstances. Members of the firm—including the Managing Director and colleagues of those who might attend the course—commented upon and helped to modify the plan for the course. At this stage the Managing Director decided to release two employees for an afternoon a week at a first course of this nature, with an arrangement for periodic review by the Department and the firm of the impact it was making. The course was started with nine members, the others being from firms in somewhat similar circumstances. Comparable courses, developed from this, have since become a regular feature of Departmental activities, and their scope has been extended to deal with the needs of larger firms.

An interesting incidental outcome of this training survey was the discovery that while the employees were eager to learn, they were inhibited from attending the course by a shyness of showing their 'ignorance' before younger college students, members of other firms, and their teacher. They tended to be overrawed by technical college premises. There developed accordingly a private arrangement, alongside the college course described above, for a more elementary class conducted in the evenings by the same teacher, but on the firm's premises.

COLLABORATION IN TEACHING

One issue of importance to the Department and current and potential 'consumers' of their services was the relative role that should be played by internal courses organized by firms themselves, and external courses given by outside teaching groups. As a contribution to the clarification of this issue, we took the opportunity offered by a large firm to attend a one-week course in 'work simplification'.

It was evident that an internal course of this kind was able to teach employees in a familiar setting, use examples known to all, and provide opportunities for developing group sentiments within the firm and for appraising staff. At the same time, it seemed that, excellent though the course was, the Department could contribute by helping to increase understanding about responses to attempts to simplify jobs.

Also, the course suggested the possibility that the existing sharpness of distinction between internal and external courses could usefully be reduced; there was a case for an interchange of lecturers between the firm and the Department and for their collaboration in the design and conduct of courses on whichever premises they were conducted. In work with firms, the Department sought increasingly to put these ideas into effect.

The Department sought closer relations with local firms in other ways also. Their efforts to show students the relation of their academic studies to their work, through discussions and project work, brought teachers and employers into closer working relation. So also did the beginnings of small-scale field research within firms by the Department. Mention has been made of the joint teaching programmes that began to develop. Senior managers worked alongside technical college teachers, lecturing to groups drawn from their own and other firms.

EMERGENCE OF A TEACHER-EXECUTIVE DEVELOPMENT PANEL

Significant changes in relations between the Department and surrounding firms occurred through our investigations into the circumstances and needs of firms and the possibilities that the Department could further satisfy the needs revealed. The very news that the research was in progress, hearing about the Department in conversation with the research team, and the experience of seeing us at work in their organizations stimulated several firms into closer relations with the Department. (This happened despite our avoidance of any attempts to advertise or 'sell' the services of the Department.) This increase of interest in the Department took such forms as offers to lecture, visits to the Department, and inquiries about courses and other services available to employees. Contact with us increased the willingness of firms to give the Department research opportunities on their own premises and their preparedness to tolerate experimentation that was novel, and sometimes confusing, to them.

During this phase of the research, two or three firms became interested enough to suggest that a meeting be held between industrial representatives like themselves, teachers in the Department, and ourselves, to discuss existing relations between the College and firms, and the work that the Department could most usefully undertake. This conference was convened by the Tavistock Institute towards the end of the project in April 1956. The detailed studies of students, an analysis of the post of Departmental teacher, and the case studies of firms had by then been completed, and some of the Department's development work was under way. The meeting was thus conducted against a background of systematic knowledge and experience, and the Tavistock Institute regarded it as an opportunity to discharge some of its obligations to those who had helped in the research.

The conference took place during one day and was held at the Tavistock Institute. It was attended by representatives of firms that had helped in the research, and by teachers in the Management Department; also by representatives of the Middlesex County Council, the Ministry of Education, the Institution of Mechanical Engineers, the British Institute of Management, the City and Guilds of London Institute, the Department of Scientific and Industrial Research, and the Tavistock Institute. Some of the information collected during the research had been circulated previously: the conference received a report on the main research findings and another from the Departmental Head on the developments being made.

Active discussion ensued on various problems of production, management, and training and on the ways in which specialists in the understanding of group and individual behaviour, in particular the Acton Management Department, could help firms. At the end of the day the meeting expressed a wish to continue contacts of the mutually productive kind experienced within the project and at the conference itself. The Chairman of the Acton

Governing Body agreed to convene a meeting at the College to discuss this.

The subsequent meeting was attended by members of the Tavistock Conference, the Acton Governing Body, the College Advisory Committee on Management Studies and Engineering, and Heads of other College Departments. Industrial representatives present gave strong support to a proposal, put together by the Chairman of the Governing Body, the Departmental Head, and ourselves, that a 'developmental panel' be formed between the Department and a few representatives of local firms to consolidate and expand the direct links that had been forged during the research.

Doubts were expressed by some members of the College staff and Governing Body about the necessity for a fresh link of this type additional to those already existing. It was explained that the research had clearly shown that communications between the Department and firms were inadequate, and that an active working partnership on live issues was necessary between Departmental teachers and representatives from local firms. This would differ from the short and formal meetings of College Governors and Advisory Committees. Whereas these two bodies represented and safeguarded interests such as those of ratepayers, elected County Council, employers, and employees, the new panel would represent, on the industrial side, actual user-firms, and would bring teacher and executive into a working partnership on practical issues important to both.

It was notable during this meeting (as on other occasions, when new information and advice is presented to an organization) that its members—i.e. members of the College and County Council—had mixed feelings towards the suggestion that something was lacking in their relations with firms and that some new arrangements were needed better to fulfil their own stated purposes.

Anxiety about the effectiveness of the College was, however, low enough to permit constructive suggestions to be made. They were to the effect that if a panel was formed it should be advisory, and should be supplemented by annual conferences like that convened by the Tavistock Institute.

Eventually, after a thorough discussion, it was decided that there would be a further meeting between members of firms and the Department, together with the College Principal, which would present proposals to the Governing Body on the possibility of a panel.

A developmental panel was subsequently formed between the Department and some of its most interested industrial users. This panel has held a series of meetings in which members have increased their understanding of industrial needs and Departmental facilities. There has been joint consideration of plans for teaching and research, of practical work for students, of subjects taught, and numbers in classes. The panel has contributed to the construction of relationships between teachers and industrial employers of a more enduring quality than had previously existed and provided opportunities for mutual learning in the course of continuous experimentation.

The College was considering, as this book went to press, the convention of the second major conference between the Department and local industry. It seems likely that the new Brunel College will set up a series of development panels in place of, or alongside, the more conventional Advisory Committees.

While representing the attempts between only one technical college department and its consumer firms to grow a living relationship between them, the developments described in this chapter clearly have wider significance and application. They provide working examples of steps that can be taken from educational administration to educational 'promotion', the necessity for which was so cogently urged at the National Conference between Industry and the Technical Colleges of May 1957.[1]

[1] See the *Report of the Second National Conference between Industry and the Technical Colleges.* Federation of British Industries, 1957.

CHAPTER VII

Increasing the Teacher's Experience and Skill

Industrial firms were critical of the calibre of technical college staff and believed that technical college salaries and conditions of work were unlikely to attract experienced and senior teachers, research workers, administrators, or 'ready-made' consultants in applied social science and production engineering. They recognized that there are exceptions. Occasionally a teacher who has the choice prefers the close contact with industry that work at a technical college promises, to the greater freedom and higher salaries of a university. Others who can choose between the College and industrial work or consultancy prefer the security, the educational work, and shorter hours of the former to the financial opportunities of the latter. Each kind of work involves a different way of life and there are some who could make a success of a university or industrial career, but prefer the work and way of life that go with a technical college. It is safe to say, however, that posts in departments of management studies and production engineering in technical colleges would not normally be a first choice for those with established reputations in social science, actual industrial management, or production engineering.

Once they embarked on more meaningful work with students and collaborative work with industry, members of the Department found that it would have been an advantage to have had more background experience or advanced training. This was only partly a matter of 'book-work' or academic training. A greater familiarity was also required with characteristic relations between a teaching, research, or consulting group and 'client' groups or organizations and with the methods that can be used to overcome field difficulties.

The teacher, research worker, or consultant needs personal or social skills of a high order in addition to scientific or academic knowledge. He needs a realistic perception of the sort of person he is and the sort of relations he makes, a high sensitivity to others, and the ability to tolerate a role to which there is always ambivalence and sometimes a good deal of outright hostility.

PSYCHO-ANALYTIC EXPERIENCE

Efforts were made by the College to secure financial help for those who wished to undertake a course of personal psycho-analysis. Such courses are expensive and can extend over years. The basis for these attempts was the belief that this experience can increase the individual's capacity to understand individual and group behaviour, to communicate with others, and to retain a balanced judgement when involved in emotionally-charged situations. It was further thought that any member of the Department undertaking analysis would be able to provide his colleagues with improved advice on the psychological aspects of their own work and help to build a culture that would support the teaching, research, and advisory services of the Department as a whole.

It was felt, however, that the undertaking of an analysis would be only one of several different qualifications for employment in the Department, and only one form of training deserving support. The most they were prepared to seek was the provision of some financial help for those who wanted it. Since analysis deals with private sectors of personal behaviour, the Department could hardly require a member to undertake it or even actively encourage anyone to do so. Two members of the staff, both social scientists, undertook personal analysis during the period covered by the study; this was not subsidised, though efforts were made to find some form of grant for them.

ADVANCED TRAINING IN HUMAN RELATIONS

The Head of the Department also inquired into the possibility of advanced training in human relations at the Tavistock Institute. We agreed that this might help to improve the quality of the Department's teaching, research, and advisory services. It seemed it would help to increase the teachers' own confidence and the confidence of firms in what they could offer. This is not to say that the services currently being offered by the Department were unsatisfactory—extra training was aimed at providing more effective services than were formally required from a technical college.

The Institute responded by devoting a proportion of the financial resources of the project to a course of twenty-five half-day sessions. At the request of the College Principal, interested persons in other departments of the College were also invited. The course aimed to give those attending access to the direct experience of senior consultants and research workers in dealing with group and individual behaviour, organization, management and personnel work. Lectures or discussions on principles of management or personnel administration were not included. An attempt was made rather to impart greater insight into the factors involved in actual field work with organizations. The curriculum consisted of seminars on Institute projects, conducted by those who had directed them, and a series of case conferences on teaching, research, and consulting problems brought by course members. Sofer acted as tutor to provide continuity between meetings and to keep the relevance of material to the course members at the focus of attention. To maximize the amount of learning, the size of the group was confined to a number suitable to face-to-face teaching where close interaction between students, and between students and teacher, is contemplated (a maximum of about twelve). Sessions were spread over an academic year so that a continuous relation could be maintained with the teaching staff over an extended period. This arrangement helped at the same time to give support from a specialist technical base to an outlying group developing new applied work in human behaviour.

The course started in September 1955 with eight members. These comprised the entire full-time staff of the Department (at the time six people) and two members of the College Department of Mechanical Engineering. During later months one member of the Department of Mechanical Engineering was unable to continue because of departmental responsibilities and one newcomer to the Management Department joined the course.

The formal teaching of the first term was mainly descriptive of the ways in which members of the Institute had undertaken research and consulting with client organizations. In a series of case conferences held concurrently, individual course members presented material, while colleagues and Institute staff discussed it with them.

There were two main types of 'case', the examination of achievements and difficulties in relations with firms and students, and the elucidation of the functioning of organizations with which course members had been connected. The second term moved towards more general work on management training schemes and processes, and on teaching and field research methods. The third term return to accounts of specific Institute projects, the ground being re-worked, since course members had assimilated previous material and could handle the concepts and tools of analysis in a more sophisticated manner.

Problems in Teaching a Mixed Group

For the greater part of the course those attending were divided fairly evenly between persons with formal qualifications in psychology and those with formal qualifications in engineering. Accordingly, one of the central problems of the course was the varying levels of familiarity with the concepts and approaches being used. The engineers were not entirely unfamiliar with these, since they had worked with their social scientist colleagues for some time. Their training was, however, in quite different disciplines, and ones that were much more concrete and tangible in subject matter.

There is, moreover, a great difference between accommodating oneself to collaboration with specialists in a field different from one's own and trying to acquire part of their expertise for oneself. Any specialized training must include, in a sense, something of a de-specializing in other areas. At times it required considerable reorientation for the engineers to accustom themselves to the systematic treatment of social and psychological material in a technical manner. This was a difficulty similar to that found by their own College students.[1]

[1] As previously mentioned, the Department was unusual in combining management studies with production engineering. This combination was on the whole an advantage. It posed in crisp form the problems of the industrial manager in applying his knowledge and experience of both physical and human resources. Also, the teaching of the Department enabled the staff to take up at appropriate points the social and psychological aspects of efforts to improve production processes.

There was by no means a complete difference of viewpoint between the engineers and the social scientists. While the ideas used in the course were much more familiar to the social scientists than to the engineers, the social scientists still had to work to assimilate these ideas and to apply them to themselves and their own work. This is always a difficult task. These inevitable difficulties, though common to the group, were borne, as it were for the group, mainly by one or two of the engineers; while it appeared on some occasions that they were holding up the progress of the rest of the group, this was also a way in which the others could listen to a repeated explanation and series of questions and answers without loss of face. This is one way, at least, in which the mixed experience of a group can help the total learning process.

Case after case was worked over in which common elements could be identified and alternative modes of approach could be assessed. This repetition at times made course members impatient; it was said that they had already been through all this before during the course, had already met it in their own experience, and were learning nothing new. At the same time, lecturers and the tutor noticed as the course went on a significant increase in the sophistication of course members in their approach to the projects and cases discussed. Course members also showed increased familiarity with the social and psychological factors they might expect to encounter in teaching, research, and consulting.

The group felt at some stages that they were being left in a state of suspended animation: they were learning to identify elements of social situations and their own 'mistakes' in dealing with them, but did not think that they had been given the means for overcoming the problems they had learned to identify. The risk of this frustrating experience is probably one important factor in the resistance of any group of students to social science teaching.

It became clear that while this kind of teaching must involve the abandonment of accustomed ideas, more has to be given to the group than has been taken away. For optimal learning, students must be convinced that there will be a net gain on the transaction. It seems necessary to make clear at the start of a course exactly how much can be expected from it. There undoubtedly existed unrealistic hopes that the course would take members much further than was possible. The course, in other words, was developmental rather than professional—in much the same way as a successful management development programme, which seeks to help the individual travel a little further and faster along a familiar road rather than to make him conform to some predetermined cast.

A major principle emphasized in the course was that learning of theoretical social science in such a mixed group proceeds fastest when the central case material relates to a problem that is experienced concretely. The most useful and best-liked lecture discussions were conducted around problems and processes of engineering production. It was in the context of discussions of this type, giving due weight to technological factors in production situations, that there was greatest receptivity to ideas about sociological and psychological factors also involved. It was also clear that the meaning of the material derived very largely from the experience that most of the group had shared with the research team in a concrete research project; this argues the necessity for concurrent practical experience with 'classroom' training in the teaching of applied social science.

Towards the end, members of the group said they felt dissatisfied, as they had not been given an integrated theory of behaviour and set of associated techniques. We have already suggested some reasons for such reactions during a course in applied social science. At the same time, it was true that the lecturers on the course had shown a similarity in outlook and approach rather than a shared possession of agreed principles of social behaviour and of specific techniques applicable to defined situations. The similarities related to the dynamics of individual personality, the nature of social processes within small groups, and regular responses of organizations to research workers and consultants. Such 'theoretical' statements and assumptions as were made constituted a selection of propositions from the wide range of sociological and psychological theories which the lecturers had found of practical value in their work, and not a set of universally agreed, interrelated, and mutually consistent principles. While the difficulty was, to some extent, that the teachers had not completely integrated their own ideas and work, it derived in part from the state of social science theory generally.

This means that students seeking to improve their theoretical equipment must, to a large extent, be taught theories rather than theory, and that students seeking concrete improvements in skill, as were the Acton teachers, must acquire an increased sensitivity to social and psychological situations and to the consequences of organizational change, rather than precise rules and formalities.

EXPERIENCE WITH THE RESEARCH TEAM

Apart from theoretical teaching on the course, members of the Department closely observed throughout the project the ways in which we, as social scientists in a research team, went about our work. They were able to gain from the experience of the Institute as an established research and consulting organization. They saw the step-by-step process through which conditions permitting research and cooperation were established with the County Council and College authorities, with local firms, and with themselves.

The reasons for the ways of work adopted were repeatedly discussed with members of the Department and their various achievements and failures were critically evaluated. As the project advanced it became a jointly conceived and conducted venture to which members of the Department and ourselves contributed in a mutually acceptable manner.

CHAPTER VIII

Research as an Active Partnership between Research Team and College

The approach adopted in the Acton project was that of collaborative research. This is a form of 'action research' or 'operational research' that aims to provide information useful to those whose collaboration is sought. The research worker supplements his technical knowledge and skill with the experience and 'know-how' of those whose participation is sought. At the same time the expectation is established that the research will help the group concerned to overcome problems with which it is faced. The prospect of help is exchanged for the research opportunity.

In addition to being collaborative in approach, the project was designed on the basis of a 'professional' relation somewhat like that between a lawyer and a client or a doctor and a patient, in that the research team guaranteed professional confidentiality in respect of research data. We gave an undertaking that no research data would be communicated to any outside party until and unless formal permission to do so had been given by the person or groups intimately concerned. We adhered rigidly to this principle. At the same time it was agreed that any parties to the research could cease participation if the project was not proceeding to their satisfaction. It was especially important to the County Council that the project should be arranged in this way so that the security of ongoing work in the Department could be maintained, and short-circuiting of existing administrative arrangements avoided. It was important to guard against unsanctioned or irresponsible publicity being given to research findings capable of critical evaluation in a political way.

THE OPENING PHASE OF FIELD WORK

From the start it was clearly understood by all parties that the research would involve members of the Department in close collaboration with a research team whose members would not only collect information but help the Department (and, where necessary, the College and the County Council) in the consideration of the practical implications of their observations.

The project had originally been requested by the Head of the Management Department. He was eager that the research team should learn about the work and problems of his Department as quickly as possible, and help him and his colleagues in the consideration of practice and policy. He was keenly interested in making arrangements that would enable us to work effectively. At the same time he wanted to protect his own role from encroachment.

Individual and group discussions with full- and part-time teachers in the Department showed reactions that were rather more mixed. Some had been consulted by the Departmental Head about the project, most had heard something about it, and a few knew little or nothing about it. There were many requests for information about its objectives, the work of the Institute, and the methods that would be employed to secure the necessary information. On the positive side, members hoped the research would provide them with information about the industrial backgrounds of their students and the practical usefulness of what they were taught. On the other hand, there was naturally some nervousness about judgements that we might make on individual efficiency and possibly communicate to others, and about the possibility that the research would throw up information indicating that the particular subject taught by a teacher was of little value to students. Staff members felt that it was obscure whether we were responsible to them or to their employers (the local authority) and whether they were really free not to cooperate if they did not wish to do so. Mention was made of the College Staff Association as a body that would wish to know exactly how staff members' interests might be affected by the research.

At a meeting of the Staff Association held to discuss the project, and attended by us, questions were asked about the nature, objectives, and methods of the project. Doubts were expressed as to its desirability. Members thought considerable risks attached to collaboration with us by the staff of the Management Department; they showed themselves anxious to protect their colleagues in the Department against damage and apprehensive lest the project 'spread' at a later stage to other departments. They wanted to know how it had originated, who had wanted it, whether reports would be made on the efficiency of individual teachers, whether the research workers were qualified through technical training or teaching experience to study technical teaching, whether staff members would be discussed with their superiors, what powers the research team possessed, and what the 'real' motivation was. A motion was proposed that the Association recommend its members not to cooperate. This was vigorously debated. Speaking against the motion, a member said that if the Management Department wanted the research and was satisfied about the way it would be done, the Association should accept this situation. The research did not directly affect other departments. There had been suspicion and fear that the project constituted an attempt by the local authority to 'get at' the staff. Assurances had been needed from the research team and had been given. The research might benefit members of the College by informing them on industrial needs. After further discussion, the motion was heavily defeated. At a further meeting the staff resolved that it noted with interest that a project was to be initiated in the Department of Management and would welcome the opportunity to study the full results and implications.

By this time the details of an operational plan had been completed with members of the Department and approval was received from the Middlesex County Council and the College Principal to proceed with the plan. Arrangements were made to submit this plan to the College Governing Body for their information and advice. We attended a meeting of this body, which had before it the operational plan, and described how it had been prepared in collaboration with the Management Department. The general blessing and interest of the Governors[1]

[1] Members of the Governing Body had already become acquainted with the proposal for a research project during negotiations with the County Council. The Governors had voiced many of the same reservations and doubts as County Council representatives, but became prepared to sanction the research once they were satisfied that the proper professional arrangements described above were to be followed during the research.

soon became clear; the desirability of the research embracing other departments was raised and the Governors asked to see interim reports. Arrangements for the sanctioning of the project by the Department and by the research organization were discussed. It was announced that a liaison committee of the County Council, the College, and the Tavistock Institute had been formed to further the objects of the research and provide a formal opportunity for any of the parties represented to intimate at any time that they did not wish to proceed further. The same held for the Tavistock Institute, which could stop the project if at any time it was decided that conditions under which the team was being permitted to work were unsatisfactory. The Governing Body then approved the plan, and stated that, so far as they were concerned, the research could proceed.

In the course of obtaining formal consent we learned much about the workings of the Department and of the organizations around it, and about the loci of power and influence. The whole structure could be observed at work upon a task—the task of getting the research under way. As important was the fact that during these negotiations and discussions the people concerned were getting to know each other. They were considering the extent to which they wished or were compelled to work together, exploring each other's attitudes and outlook, testing each other's cooperativeness, and learning the rights and obligations attached to each other's roles so far as the research was concerned. The Department, College, and County were testing our integrity and trying to make certain that we were unlikely to behave irresponsibly. A *modus vivendi* was being sought. We deliberately tried throughout this opening phase to build up a professional role whose nature and limits would be clearly understood.

We also deliberately sought occasions on which the cooperating groups—and especially the members of the Management Department with whom relations would be closest—could voice any doubts and anxieties about the research and its possible consequences. Field studies of this type characteristically make people uneasy about whether they are performing their tasks adequately, about the motives and trustworthiness of the research worker, and about the possibility that a precedent of 'rights to investigate' will be established.

At various levels of intensity these feelings are always present. They are anchored partly to real problems that may arise and partly to irrational fears. To offset such anxieties and resistances to change, we relied in the Acton project on the desire of the participants to overcome difficulties in their tasks.[1] If they had been denied, ignored, or treated merely as inconvenient administrative obstacles to the substantive study, these feelings might have simmered undetected until some particularly awkward moment—such as the moment when publication was being considered—at which they could have thwarted the whole objectives of the research. The people concerned were encouraged to ventilate their feelings from the start, so that these could be frankly discussed and the degree of reality and fantasy in them explored. Unrealistic allaying of anxieties and reassurance had to be avoided. It was helpful for staff to learn immediately that they were entitled to express their views, and that these would not be broadcast; that their attitudes were sought, understood and respected, and that concrete efforts would be made to overcome real problems that might arise in the conduct of the research, i.e. that they were not pawns to be manipulated or bugs to be avoided. It was helpful for staff to learn immediately that ticipants in the research received an opportunity to test what we said against what we did. We were immensely helped by knowing as soon as possible the attitudes to us and to our tasks, and the feelings that were aroused by systematic examination of the field and by our presence in the field. As 'intruders' (although sanctioned intruders) in a field, we affected it. Understanding of the complex of reactions surrounding our presence in the field contributed much to our understanding of the rest of the field.

THE MAIN PHASE

We turn now to our relation with the Management Department, especially with the six full-time staff members, i.e. the relation between ourselves and the group concerned during the main phase of the research, during which most of the substantive data were being collected from students, firms, and members of the Department and communicated to the latter.

We were soon busy collecting information about the Department—courses, classes, students, staff, relations with firms—

[1] See A. T. M. Wilson in introduction to *The Changing Culture of a Factory* by Elliott Jaques. London: Tavistock Publications, 1951.

which staff members helped us to gather. In some cases we asked the staff individually or in a group for particular information, or staff referred us to Departmental records. At our request, staff advised us which firms to contact and which points of special interest to follow up there. They commented on and helped in the design of a questionnaire to be completed by students. They helped us to understand the functions of the various professional institutions interested in the teaching of management studies and production engineering. Frequent discussions were by now taking place—we met members of the Department as a group at least once a week and often had other meetings with the Head of the Department or with other individual teachers. Though we did not yet have a room in the Department, we were there once or twice a week. Members of the Department began to seek advice from us, especially on the content and structure of new courses. The realization grew that we could be used for help and support, especially for advice on teaching of the social sciences. There were some slight signs of dependence on us and the related wish to receive the whole of our attention, evidenced indirectly through curiosity about what we did when not at the College, through irritation that we had not been available when something important was happening, or through requests for reports on progress.

It was helpful to teachers in the Department to explain their work and discuss problems in its execution, quite apart from the advice which they received: as Francis Bacon wrote,[1]

> 'Whoever hath his mind fraught with many thoughts, his wits and understanding do clarify and break up in the communicating and discoursing with another; he tosseth his thoughts more easily; he marshalleth them more orderly; he seeth how they look when they are turned into words; finally he waxeth wiser than himself; and that more by one man's discourse than by a day's meditation.'

Events in the main phase of the research can be illustrated from two important components a study of a course and a study of the teacher's job.

In the fourth month of the research the Head requested that we meet his staff to discuss a course in methods engineering that was just about to begin. The object of the meeting was to

[1] 'Of Friendship', *Essays,* 1597.

acquaint us with the approaches to be used by the staff and to clarify ideas on the rationale of the course and on possible benefits that might be derived by students. The staff indicated that they would like our opinion on whether they were succeeding in making the outlook of students more flexible and helping them to do a better job and whether they should improve the methods being used on the course. It was arranged that we should observe the course and report to the staff. Shortly afterwards similar help was sought with respect to a course designed for young apprentices and entitled 'Entering Industry'.

Difficulties in Reporting Back

These requests and the arrangements made for the observation of courses and reporting back convey something of the hopes and expectations of the staff and the way they looked on us. They also demonstrated the access (e.g. to the teaching-situation and to staff deliberations) that collaborative research can provide. The reporting-back phase illustrated, however, how difficult relations can become as soon as the research conclusions become implicitly critical of behaviour, and how strong resistances are aroused when changes in behaviour are suggested, even when such suggestions have been sought.

We submitted to the staff written reports on the two courses that included assessments of some of the teaching methods used and of course organization. The reports mentioned that certain revisions of methods and certain improvements in organization might be helpful to students. At the meetings to consider these reports, staff were resentful and distressed. They were worried about the possibility of the reports reaching a wider audience and about unfavourable opinions that might be formed of them. It was said that the criticisms were over-done, and that they had been based on insufficient evidence, that the conclusions reached were merely matters of opinion and that our judgement was not necessarily correct. Staff said that many of the faults pointed out were well enough known already to the teachers concerned without further comment from us. They resented, they said, being treated like students having an exercise corrected.

The reaction of the staff to the documents was not wholly unfavourable. Even at an early stage one member or another pointed out that the research would be of little value if we only praised what we saw and if the Department were prepared to accept nothing that was uncomplimentary. Group processes are often of this nature, with extreme and opposite opinions being voiced in initial stages and a more moderate mean being reached in the end. In discussions that continued intermittently over several weeks, talk gradually moved from the reactions of the staff to the documents, towards the detailed points made in them. The work of the group became more task-oriented, with the meetings concentrating more on how to improve subsequent courses. While for some time hurt feelings remained on the staff side and we continued to feel it necessary to justify our comments, a change occurred in the course of which greater agreement was reached between the staff and ourselves on the appropriateness of various kinds of teaching in different situations. The major strain on the Department appeared to be toleration of the criticism of themselves. The major strain on us was the tolerance of the ambivalence towards us that was released. A substantial contribution to a constructive outcome was made by the fact that we showed ourselves prepared to be corrected on some of our conclusions in the written reports and, even more important, to help seek remedies for the defects they had commented on. This helped in a shift from the atmosphere of a bargaining table to one of cooperation between associated groups with complementary functions, one having advisory and the other administrative (production) responsibilities.

Stabilization of Research Team—Departmental Relations

It was roughly speaking on this basis that the relations between the staff and ourselves became stabilized. There were many occasions on which the staff questioned our judgement, corrected us or disliked our findings or advice (and on which we corrected our information). But it became more or less accepted that we brought information (even unpopular information) into the Department and commented on its practical implications while the Department used what they wished of our knowledge, experience, and advice. At regular meetings we communicated in a general form, which did not reveal names of individuals, various types of research material, e.g. about the attitudes of students and firms towards the staff and what they taught, trying to time such communications and to express them in such a way that the Department would make constructive use of them. It was no use, for instance, merely to repeat a critical comment made by a firm, but better to indicate how it could have arisen and to raise questions about possible measures that might meet such criticisms.

There were usually repeated discussions of topics, involving several shifts of opinion, emphasis, and perception in the group as a whole. Everyone, ourselves included, learned together, either about situations as they existed or about barriers to change. Generally, there was some progress to group agreement on major issues. There was, inevitably, considerable sensitivity about many of the points raised. It was our technical task to try to understand staff response, to keep the project task at the focus of attention, to help in the assimilation of the material and to cope with resistance to facts or suggestions where these might improve the services of the Department but involve uncomfortable changes in behaviour. These changes were aided by the position we adopted that our task was not merely to identify, but also help to overcome, agreed obstacles to the successful operation of the Department.

As a major component of the work with the Department, we undertook a description of the post of Departmental teacher, built up step by step with the group over a period of some months. As each section of the description was completed, a draft was submitted to the staff and discussed until agreement could be reached on what was to be said in the final document. By the end of this process the staff agreed that as a result of this joint work they had come to understand more clearly the nature of the roles they occupied and the environmental forces bearing on them. They now knew more about the rights and obligations of a teacher in a Management Department, the opportunities afforded for different types of work, and the limits imposed by their environment on the activities in which they might appropriately engage.

Every six months our findings about the Department, its students, and its relations with firms were collated and summarized in a formal progress report. This was submitted in the first instance to members of the Department who screened drafts to see if they agreed to the outside communication of their contents. They were naturally concerned that these contents should not be unduly critical of them. It was, however, rarely if ever necessary to delete an unfavourable remark as we were almost invariably able to record efforts made to improve unsatisifactory situations. The Department was naturally eager to have these developments recorded. Joint work on these documents helped the Department and us to understand the issues, while the interim progress reports kept the College and County Council in touch with emerging research findings and paved the way towards a final public report.

CLOSING PHASE

Towards the end of the project we announced a plan to taper off the work gradually. Our major emphasis would now be on the writing-up of the project and clearing of documents with the Department. Field work would be reduced to a minimum. Meetings with us would be less frequent. The Department should get used to the idea of a looser relationship with us. These ideas were acceptable in principle. The staff, and particularly the Departmental Head, were eager, however, for us to see its new work, partly to report on its possible improvement and to assess and evaluate changes which had occurred within the Department during the two-year period covered by the research.

We emphasized that a major objective of the research would be frustrated if sufficient time were not left for the final writing of research reports. It was with some difficulty that a programme was agreed that involved less field contact than that to which the Departmental staff had become accustomed. This position gradually became stabilized, however, and the main first-hand contact became meetings at which documents drafted by us for communication to the Principal and the County Council and for formal publication were discussed.

By this stage it was notable that the staff were little concerned that anything indiscreet or critical might be said about them, and far more interested in seeing that our findings would be presented in a way that would maximize their influence.

CHAPTER IX

The Acton Case Study in Review Findings, Achievements and Research Methods

FINDINGS AND ACHIEVEMENTS

Preceding chapters have described the circumstances and needs of the students in the Management Department and of the firms in and around Acton that the Department tries to serve.

The Department was being used by students to improve their technical competence and paper qualifications. Some were trying to use the Department, wittingly or unwittingly, either for an extra assessment of themselves or as an 'off-centre' community where they could experiment with new ways of behaviour and try to overcome psychological barriers to promotion within themselves rather than in the outside world.

An important difference existed in the local firms between their actively expressed wants and their half-expressed or unexpressed needs. But it was inadvisable to press upon firms more training or advice than they knew they wanted lest they retreated into ultra-conservatism. The most that an 'outside' organization such as the Department could do was to demonstrate competence in familiar work, respond to requests for help, and make it plain that other services could be supplied is requested. Members of the Department had to earn the right of access and collaboration.

The Department sought an active collaboration with user-firms. This would more easily enable teacher and executive to treat the identification of training needs as a joint responsibility and to pool their knowledge and experience to meeting them. Members of the Department sought also to acquire better first-hand understanding of the organizations from which their students were drawn. It was important for teachers to supplement what they were told with what they could observe for themselves through first-hand research, training surveys, and teaching on the premises of firms.

The members of the Department did not find it easy to do more constructive work with students and firms. In the early stages of experimentation they attempted too much and too quickly. At some stages current services and administrative efficiency suffered when they did this. The new methods and services that were being considered and developed were neither fully understood by, nor fully acceptable to, the students and firms whom they were designed to serve.

Because it could not provide a ready-made staff of research workers and consultants, with all the requisite academic qualications and practical social skill, the Department was handicapped. With experience and with the information and help available through the research project, including the advanced training course on human relations in industry, considerable improvement took place. Much real 'learning' occurred in the sense of a thorough assimilation of facts (pleasant and unpleasant) with all their implications for outlook and action. It was thoroughly learned that a technical college department could not become a consulting practice, a research organization, a university department, or a psychiatric clinic, though it has many of the same demands made upon it as are made on them and although it can do a little of the work of each. The Department learned to use its existing knowledge and skills in production engineering and social science as a basis for enterprise in teaching and research. Valuable concrete developments occurred as staff adopted more modest short-term targets and confined themselves more closely to innovations consistent with their levels of skill and acceptable to students and firms. As their experience and skill developed so did the range of acceptable work increase.

Within the College, the Department formed closer relations with other departments, especially those with similar or complementary interests. Within the Department, part-time teachers were brought more closely within one teaching community so that experience could be shared and standards advance together. It improved its internal administration until it became more like a good model of what effective management could do. Where vacancies occurred, new staff members with an interest in applied social science and a desire to experiment and initiate were recruited.

The Department critically reviewed its teaching programme and drastically pruned its conventional management courses. New courses, wider in scope, yet more integrated, were designed to meet revealed industrial needs and the needs of more promising students. The student counselling service began to meet an important need that will probably become even more apparent when proposed 'sandwich courses' (aiming to alternate study and work) begin. The tutorial system tightened the administration of the Department, brought the students' 'subjects' together, and integrated day and evening studies, staff and students, in a new and closer pattern of work.

Although some early attempts failed, largely through being too ambitious, the idea of joint training reviews with industry was a good one and showed prospect of reward. Two successful training surveys were completed: one began to produce practical results in the training of junior supervisors, while the other led to consulting on work study. A certain amount of learning of social science by the engineers in the Department, and, to a lesser extent, of engineering by the social scientists, occurred. Imaginative recruitment of a member of the personnel division of a large industrial concern and a psychologist with clinical experience added to the resources and facilities of the Department. Industrial executives became more interested in the work of the Department and more prepared to collaborate in arrangements such as the developmental panel which would work towards joint arrangements for academic and practical training.

The completion of our analysis of the post of teacher, including the social context of the post and the attendant relations with students, firms, colleagues, and superiors, helped the teachers directly concerned to understand more clearly the role they occupied and the environmental forces bearing upon it. Through working on the job analysis, and repeatedly discussing its data, teachers increased their understanding of the rights, obligations, and limits of the role. At the same time, the job analysis served to clarify the opportunities their present posts and conditions of service supplied for developmental efforts of the type they wished to make and what limitations of scope existed.

New concepts were introduced among those responsible for or affected by the Department's work. New activities were initiated.

Mutually supportive 'feedback' arrangements now exist in tutorials, counselling, training surveys, collaborative teaching, and the developmental panel.

ATTITUDES AND REACTIONS OF COLLEGE[1] AND COUNTY AUTHORITIES

The Department itself made some of these changes; they were domestic. But others needed the support of the College, and its own superior administrative body, the County Council, and possibly also the Ministry of Education. A study was made of what could be done within the existing administrative framework and as much as possible was accomplished within it.

On the whole, the College and County atmosphere was favourable to experimentation and development. The appointment of the present Head of the Department expressed the willingness of the College to revalue existing practices in the teaching of management studies and the social aspects of production engineering. Further, the decision of the County Council, after careful discussion and clarification, to accept the opportunity to have an outside organization examine and help change one of its operating units, was probably without precedent among British local authorities.

Yet mixed feelings are endemic in such situations. Anxiety was expressed lest the research reports be unduly critical or lest criticisms be made without recommendations for improvement that would take realistic account of the circumstances of the County and College. It was feared that research material or the research opportunity might be used in an aggressive or irresponsible way to accuse individuals of incompetence or of reluctance to make changes. Such doubts can never be completely resolved, although professional modes of procedure in social research can do a great deal to meet them.

Any organization inviting systematic investigation of its operations is forced to face awkward questions. Some of the problems uncovered may not have been known before. Others may not have been dealt with because they were awkward. As the members of the Management Department found, the identification of a need was only the beginning of a long and difficult

[1] In this section 'the College' should be taken to mean the Principal and the Governing Body.

process of doing something to meet it. The difficulties they encountered, and still encounter, as obstacles in making a real improvement in the capacity of students to manage and in securing time and sanction for really close interaction with firms illustrates this. These difficulties would not have ensued had they been content to fulfil their nominal roles as technical college teachers.

It often seems that research creates problems, but the position is rather that it brings them to the focus of attenion.

On many occasions it was difficult for the College and County authorities to face the full implications of finding that traditional ways of work with students and firms were failing to meet many of the wants and needs of those for whose benefit they were intended. Research findings implied that if the work was to be properly executed, staff would need more liberal interpretation or relaxation of many existing regulations about teaching hours, overtime pay, and academic sessions; would require greater freedom to provide experience for students and to work out appropriate training arrangements with firms; and would need a redefinition of kinds and grading of work.[1]

It was naturally difficult for a large local authority, responsible for the spending of public money, to make changes that might affect a number of departments in different colleges on the basis of the needs of any one department and the evidence provided by a single case study. While a great deal could have been done by using more fully the flexibility and opportunities already available in Ministry regulations, even this would have involved the support of the College Principal, County Council officers, and also of representative members of the public on College and County committees. For this, clear proof would have had to be forthcoming that the new modes of behaviour attempted by the Department, or supported by the research data, would be sufficiently more successful than the old and sufficiently demonstratable to the public to justify drastic changes.

To those administering public funds such considerations are

[1] One example of the consequences of the present grading of work will serve to illustrate its disadvantages. The status of a teacher depends partly on the level of students he teaches. A junior teacher may find himself in a position where new commitments with junior industrial staff—however demanding, interesting, or helpful to them and their employees this might be—will threaten his prospects of promotion.

vital and proper. There is a profound difference in viewpoint between 'operating members' of any organization and those who have to take public responsibility for changes in the way of conducting those operations.

Preparedness for change was not eased by the occurrence of elections during the project. As a consequence there was a change in the personnel of the College Governing Body and of the main County Council committee with which the Tavistock Institute and the Department worked on research and developmental matters. A great deal of learning had to take place on each committee about the problems of the Department and the needs being highlighted by the research before constructive support could be given to new work.

One of the important factors retarding the acceptability of change was the threat to the efficiency of a part of the established work and routines of the Department caused by its over-ambitious start. It was difficult for County and College to make a positive response to new and unusual requests and to undertake extra commitments when they were already uneasy lest current work woulld be neglected for expensive innovations that were as yet unproved.

In the situation, it is not so much surprising that County and College did not accept all suggested innovations as that they accepted and cooperated in as many as they did.

Much remains to be done. There is always a danger that research becomes a substitute for action rather than a guide and stimulus. General lines of action have been indicated to the College and County from research findings. We have already emphasized the desirability of more liberal College and County regulations, practices and definitions concerning teaching hours, research work, consulting, visits to firms, and the like. Present arrangements do not provide for the proportion of time to be devoted to research and to the development of new lines of work with students that are proper to an educational establishment.

What is needed is not so much a relaxation and greater degree of permissiveness, as more active encouragement of those teachers with the competence and willingness to spend a substantial proportion of their time on collaborative work with students and firms in training, research, experimentation, and consulting. Training of teaching staff should be regarded as a continuous process, and interested staff should be given opportunities to develop professional standards of skill through training or experience in outside specialist organizations. The possibility of sessional part-time appointments on a similar basis to those of hospital consultants should be explored to make it easier to employ, and offer facilities to, part-time industrial consultants.

METHODS OF WORK

Advantages of the Collaborative Approach

The manner of the research described in this book was essentially cooperative. We regarded the Departmental staff as people with whom a study was being conducted and who might or might not decide with us to make changes in their behaviour as the study progressed.

We followed the principle that pressure for change in a group can best be established by creating a shared perception with and within the group of the need for change. It would not have been sufficient for us to collect material and point to its implications. It was necessary to involve members of the Department in the collection of the material, in the regular discussion of its implications for change, and in the assimilation of its sometimes uncomfortable short-term consequences for individual members or for the group as a whole.

We have seen what members of the Department gained from this way of work in the progressive development of their knowledge about themselves and their total situation. During the project staff members used to remark that they were now seeing more of firms and learning more about their activities and outlook, that they had altered teaching methods and courses and were developing new and existing Departmental services.

What did we as a research team gain from the collaboration? The staff of the Management Department were willing—often eager—to spend time with us and to help wherever possible with advice and suggestions. Individual teachers took us into their confidence about their doubts and problems, their relations with firms and with students, and their careers. They constantly checked the validity of our observations and contributed to a more rounded view. They added the vital component of their own subjective reactions; these were voluntary contributions of indescribably greater intimacy, complexity, elaboration, and depth than those normally available through even the guided interviews of conventional field research. When the staff tried to put to practical work the suggestions for action emerging out of discussion with us, the success or otherwise of these suggestions provided a rough check on the accuracy of the observations on which the suggestions were based. They invited us to help them make decisions and consider policy alternatives. We could—and this is rare in social research—observe decision-making in process and learn what factors entered into such decisions.

A large part of the advantage of the collaborative approach lay in the help it gave us to behave effectively. Every social investigator has experienced at least twinges of conscience in taking up respondents' time, in recording notes about the things they say and do, and in publishing research reports on them.

While our culture places a high value on scientific theory-building and discovery, we also value the freedom and privacy that must be invaded if the social scientist is to pursue his work.[1] The uneasiness of the scientist in this dilemma is dramatically reduced in intensity when he agrees to provide, as an important concomitant of the research, practical and relatively short-term benefit to the work of the group. The fact that we did this in the Acton project made it unnecessary, on the whole, to probe for information not spontaneously or willingly forthcoming. On the relatively rare occasions when such probing was necessary, this was felt to be justified (long-term scientific aims apart) by the desire of the Department for success at its job.

This was not the only way in which the research was helped by the fact that the data collected were likely to be practically useful. Few research workers are consistently content with the role of onlooker. While not all research workers are frustrated administrators, most have experienced frustration. The collaborative role provides some of the satisfactions of the administrator, by giving the research worker the opportunity to assist in the birth of administrative plans and to watch their practical effect. He is also made more careful and more responsible by the prospect that his data may lead to administrative action. He cannot make a judgement of a situation or general recommendations that do not take full account of local circumstances; he must seek to understand it sufficiently well to be able to help

[1] Our dislike of invasion of privacy is made clear in our laws of libel and trespass.

devise strategic methods for its improvement. In one sense, the familiar model of 'research' permits social 'irresponsibility' where the research worker is free to complete his work without making a single recommendation or to phrase his report in such a way that it cannot be recast into a form useful for administration.

Research is ultimately rationalized or legitimized in our culture by its long-term social utility. The collaborative approach of this project was designed to have, as well, a short-term practical utility. It became clear during the project that this facilitated communication. The effectiveness of communication of research results, like any other type of communication, is very largely dependent upon the relation between the parties involved and upon the purpose to be served by the communication. Information is more likely to be understood and applied when it is realized to be relevant to a felt need.

There was no doubt in the Acton project that the collaborative relation between the staff and ourselves, together with the utilitarian element in the research design, made the staff intensely interested in data reported back by us and led often to requests for more. This is in vivid contrast to the indifference or casual curiosity with which some groups receive information presented by social scientists, which they regard as relevant to objectives other than their own. Every academic research worker is accustomed to the reaction. 'Well, it's all very interesting, but I don't see what it means to me or how it helps me.'

The further point may be made that the continuity of the relations in the Acton project made it possible for us to communicate data at an absorbable rate over two and a half years. Data relating to real-life problems are so apt to arouse strong emotions that they become difficult to assimilate in large doses. This was illustrated, in the Acton project, by the different reactions to the reports on the two courses and on the job analysis. In the former, the gap between observation and reporting was not well judged and 'confrontation' in one long document was received by the staff as an assault. The job analysis, built up piece by piece, was a more tedious piece of work and also involved repeated discussion of emotionally-charged material. Discussion of this was, however, piecemeal and more in terms of 'what could be said' rather than in terms of 'what should or should not have been said.' By the time the document was complete the material had been 'worked through,' i.e. its emotional implications had been explored, understood, and accepted.

The continuity of the relations also brought the timing of communications more under our control. We could usually wait to pass on an item of information until the time when it was most likely to be emotionally acceptable or practically useful.

The experience of the research worker in communicating his results to those cooperating with him provides him with invaluable experience in communicating the same data to the rest of the community. We included in a document one day an incidental mention of the fact that technical colleges are often regarded as 'people's universities.' The reaction of the staff against the usual connotations of this concept was so strong as to distract attention from the issue about which this phrase had been used. This taught us vividly that it would be inadvisable to use this phrase at this point in the document if we wished the document to convey its intended message to the wider audience that it was designed to reach.

Difficulties of the Collaborative Approach

Important among the difficulties of collaborative research is the temptation for the group concerned to make the scientist into an administrator and for the scientist to succumb to it. From the viewpoint of the group, the new information produced by the investigator is a challenge to action and his advice a challenge to their administrative ability. At some point the question arises whether the scientist could move out of his advisory into an executive role and do the job better. The group may want to lean on him or, less dependently and more defensively, may want him to have a go and see how difficult it all is. And he may himself become impatient of the way they are doing the job and feel he could do it better. On the other hand, the group sometimes feels critical of the way the research worker goes about his research—they feel that his information is inaccurate, incomplete, or unfair to them, that he is not doing his job properly and they could do it better.

It is essential for both to have a clear idea of their separate roles and tasks—and of the difference between consultant and executive roles. Confusion of these inevitably leads to trouble between them and a diversion from real purposes. It is especially important for the research worker not to set himself up as a competitor of the administrator; he has to be secure and content enough with his own speciality.

There is also a possibility of external role confusion. In the Acton project it was necessary continually to distinguish research team and research organization from Department. Without such a distinction, respondents found difficulty in speaking candidly. Students hesitated at first to confide in us. They thought us indistinguishable from those with academic responsibility for them, while firms felt a certain necessity to praise, or show goodwill towards, the Department and College, and refrain from anything which might be construed as critical of its practices. Once the correct position was understood and it was realized that we would be prepared to help in positive changes, respondents became more eager to help us understand the situation and appreciate their position in it. Our attempt to dissociate ourselves from the staff was in some ways disliked by the latter. Perhaps it suggested that the reputation of the Department was not good enough for us. But the advantages of separateness seemed to be realized—our independence had to be perceived by the outside world for the information to be forthcoming that could be used by the Department.

In contact with a collaborative research team participants in a project characteristically fear manipulation, i.e. being unwittingly made to do things they do not wish to do. It is true that the influence gained by a research team makes it possible for them to manipulate. They have countless opportunities to insert the thin end of the wedge. We did, in fact, prepare the ground in advance for policy recommendations we later made. We took particular care, however, to try to ensure that we were convinced of the correctness of the action to be recommended and that the staff was in the long run likely to agree that such action was desirable.

A major difference between collaborative and certain other kinds of research is the limitation on publication. Collaborative research entails that nothing shall be published about the group unless and until they have agreed. This could result in no publication at all or in a watered-down publication that says little. From the view point of communication of results to scientific colleagues and to groups in similar situations the research could be fruitless.[1] This is a risk that must be taken.

It should not, however, be over-estimated. It is possible, as experience in the Acton project has shown, to work in such a way with the group concerned that publication of most of the data is permitted. Responsibility for the views expressed in this book rests entirely with ourselves, but permission has been secured from the groups concerned to publish the private data contained in it. It constitutes a final document completed only after they have had the opportunity to study the draft and make detailed comments. While some differences between the staff and ourselves persist about emphasis, it has been possible to make all the major points originally contemplated. Most of the modifications suggested by the staff have improved the account.

We could not be sure exactly how much we disturbed the field and exactly what it was like without us. This, however, is a difficulty endemic to field research in general rather than to collaborative research; if disturbance is inevitable the collaborative approach leaves the research worker free to discuss with respondents the difference made by his presence. In the Acton project a teacher who had invited one of us to a lecture would say so if this had made him nervous and had resulted in his adopting, or refraining from, certain behaviour.

How far could we be sure that the Acton staff group was faced with circumstances and problems similar to those of other groups? We could not. But the choice lay between studying the Acton Management Department or none. Were we to forego the research opportunity on the grounds that it was only one group and that other groups might have different problems and environments? To argue that the results would not have general validity would be to imply that far fewer consistencies exist between human organizations than social scientists believe.

It is true that the Department differed from others in its

[1] The social scientist would in this event have to content himself with the research experience in itself, or with the satisfaction of having assisted in the concrete though unpublished social change—an experience familiar to all those in consultant and advisory work of whatever kind. Ideally, this should not happen—if the collaboration has been successful, sufficient progress should have been made towards the solution of the problems of the group for them to feel tolerably comfortable about seeing in print an acount of the processes by which that stage was reached.

willingness or eagerness to be an object of study, but work with it gave us a chance to study teaching, consulting, and administration within a type of community, College, and local authority structure common to all departments irrespective of the way in which they tackle those problems,[1] and to relate these first-hand observations to more easily accessible 'background' sources of information, knowledge, and opinion.

The question might be asked whether the willingness of the group to be studied really made it so different from other groups. The difference, it seemed to us, must be one of degree. Even though the study was originated by the Department, those in it remained uneasy about some aspects of the study, while other departments would probably cooperate in more limited types of study. It was not that the Acton Department was completely unresistant to the idea of being studied, while other departments would have been completely resistant. It could be said that Acton happened to be ready for a research relation at a time when there was an opportunity for it. These considerations suggest that in large areas of social life where access by social scientists is difficult, research opportunities should be taken with the occasional exceptionally cooperative group affording an opportunity for study, in the hope that this will lead not only to a better understanding of universal characteristics of such groups, but also to a better understanding of the general reasons underlying resistance to study. Such studies may also serve as test cases to demonstrate to other groups what it is possible to do, and to reassure them against fears of the consequence of being studied.

[1] The contribution of Professor Max Gluckman in his book *The Judicial Process Among the Barotse of Northern Rhodesia* (Manchester University Press, 1955) to a better understanding of the relation between law and social organization in *any* society serves as an illustration. In the case of the anthropological field studies the societies chosen are not selected for their representativeness, yet they provide invaluable, if simplified, models of the problems with which all human societies are faced and of ways of meeting them. The Acton study taught the research team a great deal on similar lines.

CHAPTER X

Conclusions: Training for Industrial Responsibility

THE POSITION OF THE TECHNICAL COLLEGES[1]

Diversity of Students

Without radical changes, technical colleges can play only a restricted role in training students for management and for technical roles that demand an understanding of social relations.

Since the connection between the rate-payer and the technical college is direct, there is a tendency to think of admission to classes as a public right. The main criteria of eligibility for admission at technical colleges, except in a few highly congested courses, are the candidate's prior educational standard and his intellectual ability to follow the course of his choice. This often results in management classes whose educational backgrounds and standards vary so widely between a required minimum and a level well above this as to pose insuperable problems for the teacher. Some students may not have completed secondary schooling, whereas others may have university degrees.

A student may, moreover, be able to follow a course, in the sense of understanding the intellectual content of what is said,

[1] Much of what we discuss in this book applies particularly to training for management, but is relevant to training in technical specialities such as engineering, where the aim is to produce engineers capable of applying their skills effectively and responsibly. It has been suggested that conventional didactic imparting of knowledge does not produce engineers who can apply their knowledge economically and flexibly (P. P. Love. 'A Criticism of the Technical Education of Recently Qualified Engineers.' *Proceedings of the Institution of Mechanical Engineers*, 1956, Vol. 170, No. 3).

but may not have had a high enough standard of general education to be able to graft greater effectiveness in behaviour on to his knowledge and understanding.

Learning about behaviour is not only an intellectual process. Students may have personality difficulties that inhibit them from making appreciable use of a training in management studies, however intelligent they are and whatever academic educational levels they have reached.

Requirements of students vary so widely that it is impossible for a conscientious teacher to give all or even most of them what they want or need. If the claims of students were followed through, a Management Department would have simultaneously to include among its services to students those of a secondary school, a vocational guidance centre, a psychiatric clinic, and a university.

Difficulties in Recruiting Staff

It is difficult for technical colleges to recruit men with outstanding managerial or consulting ability or senior social scientists for full-time or part-time teaching. They are at a premium in operating or consulting concerns. Senior managers and consultants are paid salaries so much higher than those of full-time technical college teachers that only the exceptions will turn to full-time management teaching. Some are attracted to part-time teaching out of a sense of duty, out of a liking for such work, or by the occasional opportunity that arises for collaborative work with an unusual teaching group. But the remuneration is, at present, proportionately even lower than that for the full-time teacher. The prestige of technical colleges is not high enough to confer distinction upon those of senior rank in industry who devote a proportion of their time to such work. Social scientists of high academic standing can usually obtain, and prefer, positions at universities or in research organizations, which carry superior status, opportunities to specialize, time and positive encouragement for research and consulting, wider responsibilities, or higher salaries.

The wide range of demands upon the teacher and difficulty in recruiting suitable teaching staff go together. It is not easily acceptable for a competent man to spread himself so thinly over so many requirements of different sorts that he cannot develop his work and his reputation in a chosen area of concentrated activity. A teaching system that places its staff in an impossible position is unlikely to be able to pick and choose its staff as it would like to be able to do.

Lack of Flexibility

Basic difficulties arise from a difference in the character of industrial and commercial undertakings on the one hand, and such educational establishments as technical colleges administered by local authorities, on the other. It is in the nature of all organizations that their members become identified with their purposes and methods and defensive about the necessity for adaptation, even in a rapidly changing world. This is especially so for public institutions with some degree of permanent establishment. They are less sensitively dependent on the immediate consumers of their services for reactions to the value of their work than on the views of more distant and involuntary 'financiers' (tax-payers and rate-payers) whose representatives are concerned with economy and guarantees against risk in investment.

Industrial concerns and public organizations both ultimately depend for their existence and growth on being able to adapt to real social needs, yet the pressure for change is much greater on the former. The sanctions for failure in business are quickly communicated in a competitive market; 'feedback' of information to an educational establishment is slower and more diffuse. The first question that a firm asks about an innovation is, 'Does it pay better than the old method?'; the first question about innovation in a publically controlled educational establishment must be, 'Does it do more demonstrable good for more or less the same outlay?' The results of investment in a firm are tangible and identifiable, but the results of investment in an educational establishment, especially one for further education, are diffuse and more difficult to perceive. Private investment is voluntary, but for the tax- or rate-payer, public investment is compulsory.

The preoccupations associated with private investment are inevitably those of comparative risk-taking for differential levels of expected reward, while those associated with public investment are mainly of strict supervision and the avoidance of waste.

The public investor cannot avoid paying and cannot withdraw his money, but at least he can complain of the amount he has to give up; he can demand precise accounts and require guarantees that vigilance is being exercised in expenditure on the institution and call for periodic proof that the interests served by such expenditure are at least coincident with his own.

Technical colleges are thus obliged to conform with precisely set-out requirements and to secure permission from the elected representatives, as guardians of the public interest, before altering patterns of expenditure or conducting experiments. Elsewhere, authority for these would be delegated to operating executives. Public institutions are forced to be less flexible and adaptive and to have less scope for self-initiated change than either the private firms with which they seek to work, or the universities, with their private endowments and guaranteed degrees of autonomy.

These forces influence a technical college to preserve conservative and traditional instruction primarily designed to impart information and to lead to recognizable qualifications. This makes it easy to account to the public for their activities and 'results'.

But such approaches mean little when students seek to develop their practical managerial capacity, or effectively to apply their technical skills in organizations. There are limits to the extent to which a teacher has the right to change a student, and limits to the extent to which people can change. Yet an increase in a man's capacity to manage usually require some degree of personality change in him.

Teaching people to be actively useful in organizations especially as managers, requires freedom to design situations that help students to learn and to try out new modes of behaviour. One-way delivery of material does not produce lasting learning by the student of a kind he can make his own, nor does it encourage flexibility in the use of the information presented. Knowledge can be communicated to him by lectures, but skill cannot. Actual interaction and cooperation between teacher and student are especially important with material that has emotional or personal implications. In striving to increase his capacity to manage, it is important that a student should practise working in a group, speaking, giving advice, exercising a degree of independence in judgement and action, and himself organizing work.

Collaborative work with industrial firms is also difficult to undertake within a framework of closely regulated teaching and preparation defined in conventional terms and required for fixed numbers of hours per week.

It is not sufficient for a teacher to ask or for students or executives to explain how their organizations work, and what it and its members need. The needs of industrial organizations, like those of other living groups, are difficult to convey through explanation. The executive's membership of his firm necessarily impairs some of his objectivity. He can have only one or a few vantage points within the organization. This limits the range of observations he is able to make. Scientists always seek first-hand information and the teacher is not exempt from this rule. He should supplement the information given him by making his own observations of the workings and problems of organizations.

It is in the interests of both students and firms that the teacher learns to know the firms well and at first hand. There will always be some resentment against the outsider as the one who sets himself up to know better, especially if he does not come to know and identify himself with the firm and its tasks. There is always a threat to someone's prestige even in the need to go to the outsider and in the possibility that he or the returning student will be intolerant of the established procedures in the firm. These resentments and the anxieties of students can rarely be overcome entirely by work in a classroom, or even by occasional visits to the premises of their employers. They take time as well as skill to overcome. For successful learning, the outside teacher, therefore, must undertake sustained work with the firm. Proposed courses and experiences for students should be jointly worked out; and use must be made not only of the technical competence of the teacher, but also of the experience and first-hand knowledge of the executive. Without real learning much of the formal work of the teacher, the efforts of the student, and the detailed planning and help of his employers may be wasted.

Existing limitations on the work that can be done are the more regrettable when it is remembered that technical colleges have unique opportunities to provide a combination of academic instruction and practical industrial experience. Having close contacts with young people who have already entered their chosen occupations and now turn to them to increase their qualifications, knowledge, and skill, the colleges could play an important role in integrating academic and applied learning about behaviour and organizations at a time when students are most eager to learn. The technical college could provide a forum where industrial employees can consider their practical experience from theoretical and comparative standpoints.

Living closer to industry than universities, technical colleges could also create unique research opportunities. This is especially the case where studies can be designed to include an advisory component (which pays for the right to do research) and to produce findings of practical use to the firms concerned.

It seems that much more is needed along these lines if technical colleges are not to risk being regarded from within industry as autonomous institutions pursuing vaguely laudable ends separate and distinct from industry's own.

POSSIBLE LINES OF DEVELOPMENT

In Existing Technical Colleges

For management training we have seen that the elaborate precautions at present adopted to safeguard the investment of the tax-payer can easily become constraints which threaten the purpose of the investment. Facilities for management training can become so conservative as to defeat their own objectives.

At the same time, our study has shown that if existing regulations are liberally interpreted or relaxed when their effect on work is realistically evaluated, it is possible for a determined teaching group, together with enterprising college and local authority administrators, to make positive advances.

Similar developments are unlikely to take place spontaneously in many technical colleges. Perhaps, however, one or two departments might be chosen by the educational authorities responsible as 'developmental units' for continued research, observation, and experiment. Research is necessary not only on the work environment of students but also on the effectiveness of the teaching itself. Venables has made the important point that, while the Government has now put its money on an integration of theory and practice through sandwich courses involving alternating periods of study and industrial experience, 'the principal factors involved have not been investigated, e.g. the relative length of college/industry periods, the proportion of practical work in colleges as influenced by the industrial experience, the character and general arrangement of the industrial experience, which may be the equivalent of "walking the wards" for the doctor'[1]

Research should not replace action. What might be best is the development in technical education of something like the 'operational research' model increasingly adopted in industry. This has been exemplified, in some ways, in the combinations of research and practical experiment in the case study reported in this book. This approach permits the cautious growth of limited pilot developments with selected operational units in favourable protected environments, with the possibility of extending their more successful achievements and discarding their failures.

In Existing Universities

There is a strong case for the universities assuming a more important role in helping to educate men and women to play leading roles in industry. They have more responsibility than technical colleges for educating social leaders. This is especially so now that the scholarship system has developed to a point where most young people with the necessary capabilities can win a place in a university. Universities are able to attract funds for research and teaching in new fields, have great freedom to experiment in teaching and research methods, to choose personnel, and to make innovations capable only of long-term evaluation. They are in a position to provide the platform of broad general education on which understanding of social organization or competence in research or operational management can best be built.

Post-graduate work in the social sciences at British universities is capable of expansion. Much remains to be done to bridge the gap between the specialist university theorist and research worker and their students, on the one hand, and the outside world that is their sponsor and laboratory, on the other.

Apart from the training of specialist research workers, a gap exists in undergraduate education in many faculties whose

[1] Venables, P. F. R. 'Some Problems of Technical Education and Training.' Bulletin No. 8, November 1956, the National Foundation for Educational Research in England and Wales.

students will ultimately undertake administrative or business responsibilities.

It is not suggested that the universities should abandon any of their traditional functions of advancing the boundaries of knowledge and preparing men and women for life and social responsibility in favour of narrower vocational ends—though much vocational teaching has long been taking place in universities.

It is suggested rather that students can be better helped to understand the structure and dynamics of the society of which they are part and of the organizations in which they will work, and that preparation for life and social responsibilities will be enhanced, not diminished, thereby. Much has been heard in recent years of the increasing necessity for an 'educated man' to have the elements of the natural sciences as part of his intellectual equipment. There are good practical grounds—in the needs of industry and in the strains of modern social organization—for including elements of the behavioural sciences among those which go to make up a general education.

Additionally, there is obvious scope in the universities for post-graduate training in industrial management closely combined with appropriate academic teaching and with contact with industry through social research programmes.

In New Institutions

We have seen, in our study, the difficulties endemic in trying to meet the real needs of management training in institutions designed mainly for very different kind of learning. It takes a rare group of teachers and an enterprising college and local authority to venture from such an established institution into education for what is essentially more effective personal behaviour in organizations. Together the Acton teachers and the College and County authorities found it necessary to use every ounce of play in their regulations and sanctioning system, and even then the amount of progress they could make was haltered by the design of their institution and the needs of the external world.

There exists an acute need for management training institutions—wherever they are located—with something of the authority, standards, and conditions of work of a university and with a preparedness to enter into an active partnership with industrial firms in meeting their needs and those of their staff. These institutions will need to take into full account the advances in applied psychology and sociology which are now taking place not only in public educational institutions, but also to a significant extent outside them in private firms, research organizations, independent scientific and training institutions, and industrial consulting practices. These advances highlight the fact that working groups commonly accept unnecessarily low levels of achievement but can be brought to release the potential which lies within them. There is clearly an unsatisfied need for a sophisticated form of education for management based on a combination of background academic teaching, 'operational' teaching by industrial managers, participation in systematic investigations of social and industrial problems and processes, and increasing executive responsibility under joint academic and practical supervision.

It may be that management studies will receive new opportunities in the small number of technical colleges that the Government is now developing as 'advanced colleges of technology'. These are evidently to have more freedom and independence, both academic and administrative, than the ordinary college. It should be easier in new institutions to make the necessary breaks with tradition, precedent, and self-limiting conservatism whose effects we have described.

It remains to be seen whether the innovations will go far enough in the opportunities and conditions provided for the advancement of management studies. More rapid progress may be made within the existing universities, may have to await the inception of a new technological university, or may require the emergence of some quite new form of institution.

It is possible that the adaptation and development of existing educational institutions will not be enough. Thinking and experiment so far have been restricted by the assumption that existing institutions can do the job required or can be fairly simply adapted to do it. It may be advisable to consider the problem of management training from the other end—to work back from training needs within firms and other operating organizations to the design of training institutions likely to be able to meet those needs. The needs of organizations and of those who man them are wide, deep, and constantly changing, and the attempt of educationists to meet those needs will involve a marriage of two worlds long thought incompatible. If improved training for management is to be given the degree of priority that our total social situation demands, it will be necessary to locate and staff new institutions at those points in the social structure where restrictive tradition, established academic interest, and self-limiting regulation are at a minimum and opportunities for experiment, influence, high-level staffing, and collaboration are at a maximum.

SELECT BIBLIOGRAPHY

Articles and Papers

Editorial Articles in *The Technical Journal* (the organ of the Association of Teachers in Technical Institutions).

SOFER, C. 'Organization and Training in a Small Firm.' *The Manager*, Vol. 25, No. 7, pp. 563-9, July 1957.

WILSON, A. T. M. 'A Note on the Social Sanctions of Social Research.' *Sociological Review*, Vol. III, No. 1, pp. 109-116, 1955.

WILSON, A. T. M. 'The Background of Management.' *The Manager*, pp. 699-701, September, 1957.

VENABLES, P. F. R. 'Some Problems of Technical Education and Training.' *National Foundation for Educational Research Bulletin*, No. 8, 1956.

Reports and Memoranda

BOARD OF TRADE (Bailleau Committee). *A Central Institute of Management*. Report. London. H.M.S.O., 1946.

FEDERATION OF BRITISH INDUSTRIES. *Report of the Second National Conference between Industry and the Technical Colleges*. London, F.B.I., 1957.

MINISTRY OF EDUCATION (Percy Committee). *Higher Technological Education*. Report. London: H.M.S.O., 1945.

MINISTRY OF EDUCATION (Urwick Committee). *Education for Management*. Report. London: H.M.S.O., 1947.

MINISTRY OF EDUCATION. *Technical Education*. CMD 9703. London: H.M.S.O., Feb. 1956.

PARLIAMENTARY AND SCIENTIFIC COMMITTEE. *Memorandum on Higher Technological Education*. London: H.M.S.O., July 1954.

Books

GOODMAN, L. LANGDON. *Man and Automation*. Harmondsworth: Penguin Books, 1957.

URWICK, L. F. Introduction to Newman, Harry, and Sidney, D.M., *Management Teaching*. London: Routledge & Kegan Paul, 1955.

VENABLES, P. F. R. *Technical Education*. London: Bell, 1955.

WILSON, A. T. M. Introduction to Jaques, Elliott, *The Changing Culture of a Factory*. London: Tavistock Publications, 1951.

INDEX

For Product Safety Concerns and Information please contact our EU
representative GPSR@taylorandfrancis.com
Taylor & Francis Verlag GmbH, Kaufingerstraße 24, 80331 München, Germany

www.ingramcontent.com/pod-product-compliance
Ingram Content Group UK Ltd.
Pitfield, Milton Keynes, MK11 3LW, UK
UKHW022109190926
475702UK00013B/1340

* 9 7 8 1 1 3 8 8 6 3 7 7 4 *